Johnny Kingdom's West Country Tales

www.**rbooks**.co.uk

Also by Johnny Kingdom

Johnny Kingdom: A Wild Life on Exmoor
Bambi and Me

For more information on Johnny Kingdom and his
books, see his website at www.johnnykingdom.co.uk

Johnny Kingdom's West Country Tales

Johnny Kingdom

BANTAM PRESS

LONDON • TORONTO • SYDNEY • AUCKLAND • JOHANNESBURG

TRANSWORLD PUBLISHERS
61–63 Uxbridge Road, London W5 5SA
A Random House Group Company
www.rbooks.co.uk

First published in Great Britain
in 2011 by Bantam Press
an imprint of Transworld Publishers

A CIP catalogue record for this book
is available from the British Library.

ISBN 9780593066522

Addresses for Random House Group Ltd companies outside the UK
can be found at: www.randomhouse.co.uk
The Random House Group Ltd Reg. No. 954009

The Random House Group Ltd supports the Forest Stewardship
Council (FSC), the leading international forest-certification
organization. All our titles that are printed on Greenpeace-approved
FSC-certified paper carry the FSC logo.
Our paper procurement policy can be found at
www.rbooks.co.uk/environment

Typeset in 10/15.5pt Versailles by
Falcon Oast Graphic Art Ltd.
Printed and bound in Great Britain by
CPI Group (UK) Ltd, Croydon, CR0 4YY

4 6 8 10 9 7 5

Mixed Sources
Product group from well-managed
forests and other controlled sources
www.fsc.org Cert no. TT-COC-2139
FSC   © 1996 Forest Stewardship Council

I'd like to dedicate this book to my two sons,
Stuart and Craig, my grandson, Harry,
and my great-grandson, Spike,
who are very special to us.

Contents

CHAPTER 1

Owls and Goblins

YESTERDAY I WENT OVER TO THE OTHER SIDE OF EXMOOR TO VISIT Aunt Ada. She's ninety-seven now and still bright as a spark. Now every time I come along to see her in the residential home, the pretty nurse there always brings out the tea things. She knows my auntie and me are fond of a cuppa so we get one straightaway.

The first time I came to see her there, a few years back, the tea came, Aunt Ada took a sip and made a face. I asked what was wrong. She wrinkled her nose. 'This tea tastes like gnat's water,' she said.

I had a swallow then nodded my head. 'Like pee, right?' I agreed.

She drew herself up and looked me in the eye. 'No,' she said, correcting me with a fierce stare, 'like gnat's water.'

Ever since that time, whenever I come visit, she says the same thing: 'This tea tastes like gnat's water.'

Each time I answer, 'Like pee, right?' and she gives me that same old indignant look. 'No. Like gnat's water.'

Well, this time we went through it all again, though the tea tasted just fine to me, like it always does. To Aunt Ada, too, for she drank the lot, as she always does. And when she'd finished, she started telling me one of her stories again, the old stories she'd been telling for years. Some were true stories of the old days, and some were myths and legends from the West Country, tales that had been told to her by her own parents and grandparents.

This one story was about the goblins that used to terrify the workers down the tin mines on Dartmoor, a long time ago. Tin mining began on Dartmoor as early as pre-Roman times and didn't stop until the twentieth century. Because it was fairly easy to mine the tin at first, underground work didn't start until the eighteenth and nineteenth centuries, and it's in these underground mines that the legend comes from, I reckon. Those old miners, down there in the dark where it must have been scary as hell, used to hear strange sounds, noises, that they called 'the knockers'. I guess that's because the sounds were like someone knocking on wood or some such. They were thought to be made by goblins that were rarely seen, but always heard. Sometimes they were good, sometimes bad. When they were in a kind-hearted mood, they helped the miners no end. They'd give a few knocks to guide the men, often to warn them of a danger ahead. Or they'd guide the miners to a rich seam so that they knew where to dig.

Now this happened only if, for some reason, the goblins happened to like particular miners. Some men considered themselves well favoured by these goblins, particularly if they kept avoiding danger or had lucky digs.

But, oh my, when the goblins were in a bad mood, or if they took against any of the miners, they were horrid. They'd steal candles so that the poor miners would be left in the dark. Or they would hide away picks and other equipment. Sometimes it seemed they were being plain mischievous, at other times just plain nasty, like breaking the pick instead of hiding it. On those days, when the men feared that those unseen creatures were in a sulk about something, they did their work in fearful silence, let me tell you.

'But y'know, Johnny,' Aunt Ada said as she wound down her story, 'those miners, if they were clever, could always get the knockers on their side. It's like us ordinary folk, ain't it? If you want someone on your side, you just got to be nice to 'em. And they'll be nice back, most likely.'

And that was what some of the miners did. Left out a bit of pasty for those goblins every day, or maybe even a drop of cider in the bottom of a cup. And from then on, those men would hope the knockers would look kindly on them, and guide them out of danger in those difficult underground places.

*

I listened to Aunt Ada, like I always did, and loved hearing those stories all over again. They were part of our history, if you know what I mean. But when the visit was over and I got back into my jeep, I got to thinking. Aunt Ada is nearly a hundred now, and the last of those old girls, my gran's daughters. How many more times would I hear her stories?

And, for that matter, how long would I be around, to tell of Aunt Ada, and of others, of the wonderful people I've known, and the tales they had to tell. I'm seventy-one now, and I hope God will give me some more good years. But after I go, who will tell of the family and friends, of their way of life now gone, of their stories?

I thought about this all the way home. That evening, Julie, my wife, saw I was brooding. Now Julie and me, we've been married well over forty years, nearer fifty as a matter of fact, so she knows me well enough, I'd say. So I told her what was troubling me. 'Johnny,' she said when I'd finished, 'you should write it all down. Get it into a book, those old stories. Keep them alive, for our kids and grandkids, and anyone else who might be interested.'

So that's how it started.

The day after my visit to Aunt Ida, the rain came down in bucketloads. I had intended to take my camera out to try to get a photo of the cuckoo, something I'd not yet done. I've taken photos of every kind of wildlife up here on Exmoor, but I've never got one of the cuckoo.

But the wind was blowing the heavy old branches in the trees, and the rain was so torrential you couldn't see your hand in front of your face. Looked more like November than April. My chances of spotting the cuckoo were not too good.

Besides, I was still thinking of Aunt Ada. And then her sister, who was my mum; and their mum, my grandma. All of them gone now, and only Aunt Ada left.

Julie came into my tiny office in the back of the house. It's full of my books and DVDs and photos I've taken, as well as several pairs of red stag antlers and a stuffed falcon someone gave me that looks real enough to scare the bejesus out of anyone stumbling into it in the dark. I was sitting there, staring outside at the rain. Still thinking, still brooding.

Julie asked if she should make a pot of tea, and I started to nod. But, instead, suddenly I jumped up and grabbed her hand. 'Come on, get on some waterproofs and your boots. We're going out.'

She asked where to, and I had to admit I wasn't sure, not then. But something was driving me. It was as if all the old folk who were gone now, folk I knew and loved, were clamouring around in my head shouting to be heard. To tell their old stories.

They were like ghosts, haunting me.

By the time Julie had got into the jeep and I had started the motor, I knew where I was going.

'Home,' I said. 'I'm going home.'

It wasn't far. Just a few miles along the Bray Valley on the edge of Exmoor, before cutting up the hill to High Bray, the village where I was born. Not far, but a lifetime away.

It's a beautiful valley, even on a day like that, the rain torrential, the wind howling like a hound dog. Woodland for miles, following the River Bray around the curves of the hills. Normally, in April it's an idyllic sight, the river all peaceful and lovely, the sun shining on it, the trees starting to get ready to burst out in green. Many a day and night I've poached salmon and trout from that river, though not for many years, only when I was young and when it was the only way to feed the family.

Today, though, the river was roaring over its banks, flooding the grassy fields of the valleys, swirling like hell around the old oak and beech and ash trees. 'I don't recall ever seeing it so high,' Julie said, and I had to agree with her. Quite a sight, it was.

I drove on through the rain and we passed the quarry where I used to work as a young man, and the hill I used to walk down on my way to work. I turned the jeep on to a narrow road going up to Brayford, the little village before mine. Here was the shop where we used to nick sweets and soft drinks and, later, when we were older, cider off the old couple who ran it. All us kids did it then, mind, only no one likes to admit it now that we're grown and have families of our own. But times were hard then; it was right after the war, food was still scarce. I don't mind talking about it because it was a long time ago. I was a terror then, but so were all my mates. That's the way it was then.

I drove the jeep slowly out of Brayford, up the hill to

High Bray, or Bray Town, as we called it. The rain was still driving down and I was talking up a storm as well, the windows wide open so I could point out things to Julie. 'Over there, see? Well I never, the old telephone box is still there.' I started laughing so hard I stalled the car. 'I got fond memories of that phone box,' I said when I got going again. 'I used to kiss the girls in there.'

Julie didn't look too impressed, so I took her hand, keeping one on the steering wheel. 'Don't worry, darling. That was before I met you, for sure.'

'Johnny, all I'm worried about right now is catching my death in this wet and cold – shut the windows before I'm soaked to my skin,' she replied.

I noticed then that the rain was driving in on her so I shut the windows quick and put on some heat as we drove out of Brayford and up to Bray Town.

It's only a small place, not even a pub or a shop, never was, even all those years ago. 'Look, Julie, there's where my gran lived. Aunt Ada's mum, as well as my mum's mum. I loved my old gran and that's a fact.' I grew pensive for a moment, thinking of her. I spent a lot of time in that house with my gran.

Julie put her hand on my knee and gave it a pat. 'I know you did, Johnny.' She smiled at me. She's heard all this before, but she always listens again. It's only one of the many reasons I love her so much.

I kept thinking of my grandma, and how it was when she died. She was all laid out upstairs on the bed and I was brought up to have a look at her, to say goodbye, as was done in those days. Around her head and tied under her chin was a white band with a button on top, and in front of her feet were two concrete blocks. I said to my dad, 'What's all that for?'

'The band around her head is to keep her mouth from flopping open,' he told me, 'and the concrete is to keep her feet so they stay up, don't fall down.'

'Why does that matter?' I asked him. 'Keeping her feet straight?'

'T'would add another foot to the coffin, boy, if they weren't up. You got to think of these things, y'know.'

Things were certainly done different in those days.

Julie and I stayed in the jeep for some time, me gazing at my gran's old home, remembering. She had a huge open fireplace, with kettles and pots and pokers and all sorts of metal objects hanging up in there. It wasn't just for warmth, that fire. It was the hub of the house.

My uncle, who is quite a character and has many good tales, likes to tell of how he used to keep the fire alight when he was a lad. It had to keep going night and day some weeks, to keep the damp out, dry the clothes, boil the kettle. It was his job to make sure it didn't go out yet didn't flare up too much and burn all our wood too quickly. So the way he did it was to always have what he called a back stick, which was a log placed at the back of the fireplace. This kept the fire in its place, as he used to say.

Well, one time he went out into the woods looking for the perfect back stick, as it was a period of cold winds and rain so there was lots of sodden clothes to dry out. 'I got a back stick like a small bledy tree,' he told us. 'And you know, that log simmered day and night for fourteen days.' He shook his head in awe. 'Fourteen days,' he repeated, 'that log burned.' Us kids listening to this story clucked and chuckled in wonder too, but we were waiting for the next part of it – the best bit.

My uncle went on, a twinkle in his eye: 'At the end of fourteen days and fourteen nights, the log finally stopped burning. And you know what happened then?'

No matter how many times we'd heard this tale, we shook our heads.

'A flippin' flapping tawny owl flew out!' he cried.

We hooted. We loved this story. 'Yep, that's what happened there in Gran's house, right in that fireplace, boys. After fourteen days hid away, no doubt scared as shit, that tawny owl survived and flew out at us, soon as that log stopped burning. The owl was still flying and flapping about so we let it out, and it's probably perched right in that tree outside the window, recalling its adventure and telling it to its grandchildren.'

Telling of that tawny owl reminds me of many of the old stories, the sayings about that night bird. Hearing the screech of an owl was always a bad sign. Someone was going to die, maybe, or something nasty was going to happen. You can understand why, I suppose, if on a dark night you heard the noises they can make. They sound fearsome, and look fearsome too, swooping down through a black sky with those great wings and those two tufts of feathers on their heads like the devil's horns.

There's an old story I heard about a farmer who went out to his fields one day to find one of his workers there dressed in a black suit instead of his work clothes. Knowing the worker's missus was gravely ill, the farmer gave the worker his condolences, thinking she'd passed away and the man was off to her funeral. 'Oh, she ain't dead yet,' the farm worker said, 'but I heard the owl screeching last night so she'll be gone by nightfall.'

The many myths there are about owls are not just from the West Country. In fact, I believe the one about owls' eggs being a cure for drunkenness is fairly widespread. And it seems that, long ago, young children were given raw or hard-boiled owl's eggs to eat in the hope they'd stop them from imbibing too much of that old beer or cider when they got grown. I bet the pub owners in those days weren't too fond of owls!

One tale really makes me laugh, though. It was said that you can get an owl to strangle itself if you go round and round a tree where the bird is perched. The owl will follow you with its big wide eyes until it wrings his own neck and his head falls off. Of course, an owl can't turn his head around in a complete circle, but it must have looked like that to lots of people, because it can turn its head quite far around, and fast too.

Owls also have the reputation of being wise. It's either one thing or the other in the stories – they're either creatures of doom and bad news, or wise old birds. I've heard tell that, in our part of the world, it has always been believed that owls are omens of evil because that's what the Romans thought, and so that's where our beliefs about the bird come from. But the Greeks, on the other hand, believed the owl was good and wise. So I guess if they had come over to England instead of the Romans, we'd have thought it a good omen instead of a bad one when that old bird hooted!

Barn owls can look particularly spooky, white like spirits. The way they dive down on their prey, silent and glider-like, can only have added to the superstitions that they were the bringers of death. They used to be called ghost owls because of their white faces and great white wings. You can see why folk in olden times were frightened of them, if they met them suddenly on a dark night. They've been with us a long time. Fossil records date back two million years, would you believe. Unfortunately, between the 1950s and the 1980s, the population of barn owls dropped 70 per cent, down to only four thousand pairs. But I believe the numbers are on the rise now, thanks to conservation groups and other like-minded people. It would be a sad thing if the barn owl disappeared altogether. I'm hopeful that it never will.

CHURCH BELLS AND BATS

CHAPTER 2

Church Bells and Bats

AFTER LOOKING ABOUT THE HOUSE WHERE I WAS BORN, THE LAST in a row of cottages on the square, and reminiscing about my dad's garden – he was a grand gardener, and won prizes for his produce – Julie and I poked about the sheds behind the house, where the toilets used to be. The toilets weren't there now, of course, but the sheds were filled with old tyres and whatnot.

'I wonder who lives here now,' Julie said. 'Maybe we shouldn't be plodding about in their back garden.'

But no one was around; no one bothered us. I stood looking at where Dad's garden had been, now a wasted bit of ground, and thought how sad he would be, being so proud of his garden. But the view across the Bray Valley was as grand as it had ever been, the fields starting to green up after the long winter, the rainclouds rolling across the sky above just as I remembered. It looked the same as it did over seventy years ago when I first laid eyes on it.

After the house and garden, Julie and I went to the church, which is right opposite the house where I was born. This was where I first started work with my dad as a gravedigger. I buried many folk here, including my own parents, who are there now. I dug many a grave in this very churchyard, stood around for hours watching folk bury their dead.

I remember how us gravediggers used to hate the Methodist funerals. We'd hide ourselves discreetly behind a tree or a beech hedgerow, waiting for the prayers and suchlike to be over so we could finish our jobs. The Church of England lot, they were fine, no problem. The vicar would briskly say a prayer or two and the mourners would say their goodbyes to their loved ones not exactly in a rush, but not lingering a moment more than necessary either. They were eager to get to the wake and a drink or two. But the Methodists – well, they did go on. The pastor would pray for hours, it seemed, and when he finished it wasn't over. Oh no, not a bit of it. No one would move! Not for ages. They hung about, peering down into the grave, talking sombre-like in hushed voices, keeping us poor gravediggers hanging about for hours when all we wanted was to fill in the graves and get on home to a hot dinner and maybe a well-earned drop of cider. But no, those Methodists weren't in any hurry to leave. Maybe their wakes were a dreary affair, nothing but a cup of weak tea and a dry biscuit. Who knows?

I only know how the gravediggers felt, and I tell you this, when I go to a funeral I get away from the church-yard as soon as I can, out of respect to the men who have to finish the job.

The rain was getting worse, if that was possible, so Julie and I ran into the church. God knows, it was good to be back there in that place. I used to sing in the choir when I was a boy. I've always been a believer, despite my wild youth. I got up to a lot of mischief, but I know God is forgiving and I never have lost my faith.

But I have to admit that we did get up to some mischief in the church. In those days, all the men wore hats and, before going into the church, they took them off and hung them on a bunch of pegs on the wall of the church porch. Each man had his own peg. One Sunday, me and some of the other choir boys sneaked out during the service and changed the hats around. When the men came out, they automatically grabbed the hat from their own peg, not realizing the hats had been switched. I can tell you there was a lot of swearing and cursing going on in the church-yard when they started to realize they had the wrong hats on!

Julie hadn't heard that story, and had a right laugh when I told her. 'There was one man there, Ned Walker, what a sod he was. He couldn't see the fun of it, went about trying to find us choir boys to thrash the living daylights out of us. I tell you, we ran the he— Whoops!' I stopped and put my hand over my mouth.

'What's the matter?' Julie asked.

'I shouldn't be swearing in church. It reminds me of that story about the ghost bells coming out of the sea, down Cornwall way.'

'What bells?'

'Church bells, just like those in this here church. The story goes that, long ago, some bells were being brought by ship to go in this village church by the sea. But on the way the captain of that ship started swearing about something, and the ship went down into the rough sea. Those bells can be heard on a rough and stormy night to this day.'

Julie was smiling. 'It's a good story. That captain must have had some good swear words on him.'

'Yeah, but now I think on it, maybe God doesn't mind the word "hell". So, as I was saying, us boys ran the hell out of there, let me tell you. But we ran away sniggering all the same.'

Back out in the porch of the church, I started having a peep behind the notice boards hung up on the stone walls. 'What're you looking for?' Julie wanted to know.

'When I was a choir boy, I used to look behind these things every Sunday. Used to be bats there. Like as not, still are. Bats love hidey-holes like this.'

No bats this time, though. Like I did in the old days, I looked into every crack and crevice, each tiny hole in that porch, but there was nothing there, only ancient cobwebs. But the ghost of my young self was there, believe me, poking about looking for bats, interested in wildlife even then, before I had a clue what life would bring about for me.

Though I like bats, not everyone does. According to all the old superstitions about them, they weren't too well liked at all. I suppose it's because, like the owl, they're nocturnal. Long ago, people were wary of the dark, if not downright frightened of it. All sorts of mysterious things were said to happen in the dark, and not only do bats come out at night but they look like some creature that's half bird, half mammal, with a furry body and bald leathery wings but a face that's almost human.

Bats were also associated with witches and Hallowe'en and suchlike. And women were afraid of bats because it was said they got tangled up in a woman's hair if she got too close. I've never known that to happen, but I can see how folk believed it. If a bat can't see where it's going, well, it could get tangled up any old place, can't it!

I did hear a spooky tale of a woman who hid under her kitchen table when a bat swooped into the room through an open window. She was so terrified she wouldn't get out until the bat flew off. Unluckily for her, the bat stuck around, flapping about looking for the way out and ending up hanging from the curtain rail. Now this was many years ago and the woman lived alone. There was no such thing as telephones and suchlike then. The story goes that she stayed there for five days and five nights, and so did the bat, each wanting the other to get the hell out of there. But here's the strange thing – the bat finally had enough. He flew down right under that kitchen table and, sure enough, got tangled in her hair just like in the old stories. The woman nearly died of fright, but because the bat was a magic one, it turned her into a witch. Instead of being afraid of the bat, she now saw it as her friend and very carefully disentangled the creature from her long, dark hair.

After that, when folk came to her cottage, they noticed a whole family of bats living inside the kitchen. At first they didn't think much of it, for she'd always been a strange sort. But then, after a time, they noticed that, every week, there were more and more bats. And, at the same time, travellers coming through the village began to disappear. Oh my, did that put the fear of God up the good people! They put two and two together and figured the witch was changing the missing travellers into bats.

After that, not a soul came near that cottage again. And for years and years, the villagers told their children that if they roamed too far from home, and went too near the old woman's cottage, the witch would turn them into bats.

The rain had settled into one of those heavy drizzles and fog so beloved of these Exmoor hills as we left the church. Heading back to the jeep, I remembered all those graves I dug in weather like this, and worse, too – snow and hail, freezing cold as well as killing rain.

There are many tales of strange things happening in churchyards. An old man I know who used to live up Dorset way told me of a village church there that was haunted by a teenage boy who'd been found dead there in the early 1700s. He was known to have had fits and everyone thought his death was brought on by those, so he was buried straightaway without an inquest.

The thing is, that poor lad had been strangled, and no one knew, so the killer had got away with it. As you can imagine, his ghost was bloody unhappy. One day, this boy's mates were out playing around the churchyard when they heard strange noises coming from somewhere amongst the graves. They followed the sounds until, suddenly, the ghost of the dead lad was standing in front of them, pointing to his grave! They turned and ran like hell, straight to the magistrate's house. They were convinced the ghost had been trying to tell them something and, luckily, they were listened to, for the body was exhumed and examined and they realized it was a murder, not a natural death.

According to the story, the murderer was never found, but the boy's ghost must have been a little bit eased, for he never appeared again. But they say his strange cries can still be heard sometimes in the church.

I told Julie this story as we drove home, glad to get out of the rain and at the thought of having a hot drink and a bit of warming food. When we'd got home and were dry and cosy again, I said, 'I keep thinking of all those old stories, you know. The people who passed them down, year after year. All the ones folk have told me over time, the ones I heard when I was a boy. Some true stories, and the others, too – all those myths and legends that have come out of the West Country. So many.'

Julie nodded. We spent the rest of the evening talking and laughing about the things we used to do, and the tales we used to tell. It was a good evening, and made me more determined than ever to get all these stories down.

CHAPTER 3

An Old Horse and Cart

THE RAIN CLEARED AT LAST, AND A GOOD THING TOO, FOR IT WAS already mid-afternoon. Time to get my camera, forget about stories for the minute and concentrate on the wildlife, for after all that's my job, taking photos, making films of Exmoor.

So I kissed Julie, grabbed my stuff and set off in the jeep to our land, the 52 acres on Exmoor I was able to buy when my television series for the BBC took off. That's where I love to be, sat there in the hide waiting for a red deer or a badger to appear.

And that's just what I did. It wasn't until the next day that I started thinking about the old stories again. I'd been thinking about change, about how the old ways of living have mostly disappeared. I know that's the way things are, how they've got to be, and I know too that some of the changes are for the good. Life was tough when I was a lad, bloody tough, and I like to think it's a bit easier for youngsters today, that maybe life isn't so tough that they've got to poach for food.

But not all the changes are good. I love Exmoor, it's where I live and work, and where I've always gone when I'm in a spot of bother, need to think, unwind. It soothes me, the wildness of it, the beauty of the land. But the other day, when I was up to Anstey Common, I found an empty bottle of whiskey and a half-dozen empty beer cans lying about.

I couldn't believe my eyes, seeing that. Anstey Common is on Exmoor, in a fairly isolated spot. It's remote and out of the way of most day trippers and such-like. Anstey Common is at the top of a deep valley with a woodland of old withy, scrub oak and silver birch. Up on the common it's a grand view; you can look all around you to see rolling hills, green fields and valleys one way, rough uncultivated ground in another direction. I've been going up to Anstey Common for years, and I was there that day with my camera hoping to get a shot of the cuckoo. I'd heard it there only a few days back, calling out in the early morning, the moor quiet except for that cuckoo, and not a soul out amongst the yellow gorse and colm grass but me. Though late April, there'd been a frost in the night, but the day was warming up nicely, the sun shining its head off on the leafless silver birch, the hawthorn, the beech along the hedgerows. All about to come out in bloom, any day now.

Today would be the day, I could feel it in my bones, when I'd get my photo of that cuckoo, I thought as I got out of my jeep and started to walk across the rough mossy grass of the common.

That's when I saw those bloody beer cans. Scattered all over the ground. And the empty whiskey bottle, tossed into the heather.

Now, as anyone who knows me will tell you, I've nothing against having a drop or two; and in my youth I could drink anyone under the table. But even in my wildest moments I didn't throw my empty cider bottles all over the countryside. I grew up with respect for the land, for it provided our food, our livelihood and a place to live, to roam, to enjoy. Those tossed beer cans, that whiskey bottle thrown carelessly away on the moor, showed disrespect for Exmoor and all the folk who live on it and love it.

It's a bit like those who come to live here and then want to change it. Like those I know who complain because the cock crowing next door disturbs their sleep or the smell of good honest dung makes them ill. I'd welcome anyone to come and live here, as long as they understand where they're coming to and don't try to change our ways.

'That's the sort of changes we don't bloody need,' I said out loud, thinking about these things after I'd gone home.

Julie had come into my cluttered but cosy office, where I was sorting out some of my photographs. 'What changes?' she asked.

'You know the sort. Litter all over Exmoor. Post offices

closing. Village shops going fast. New people fussing over the stuff that makes the countryside what it is, like moaning if the sheep baa too loud at night.'

'Or roaring through the centre of town at double the speed limit.' Julie shook her head. There'd been a spot of trouble over reckless driving lately.

I said, 'Julie, now that's nothing new.'

'What d'you mean?'

'Well, crazy driving and all. Remember your grandfather?'

She began to laugh, and so did I, thinking of her grandfather William. 'Now there's one of the old stories for you, Johnny,' she said.

I knew exactly which story she meant. William and his horse and cart, how he drove his eight kids around in it everywhere.

Julie's grandfather was a fine old man but, oh my, he had a mind of his own. They lived out in the country and went everywhere on the rickety old cart he had, pulled by his solid, slow, old brown cart horse.

On stormy days when the children would have got a right soaking if they'd have walked to school – it was a good few miles to the village school – William got them into that old cart of his to drive them in. And, on market days, he drove all his kids into town so that they could run about and see their friends. It was a big day out, market day.

The one time he got stopped by the police, though, he had only four of his youngsters riding in the cart as they were on their way home from market day. Now, like many of the local men, William liked a drop of cider every now and again, and even home-brewed his own. That day had been a fine market day, and a whole lot of cider had been drunk by a great many of the men, William being no exception.

The local policeman spotted him weaving up and down the one main street of the town and called out for him to stop at once. 'William,' he hollered as he grabbed the horse's reins and hung on tight to stop William from moving on, 'I can tell you've been drinking. Your driving is all over the place.'

Now that William, the cider was making him sway side to side on his perch on the front of the cart, but he straightened his shoulders quick as a flash and did his utmost to sit steady on his seat. 'Well now, Martin,' he said, enunciating every word as clear as he could, 'I may have had a pint or two, I have to admit.' Unfortunately for him, he couldn't help slurring the last few words, and the cider on his breath was so darn powerful it nearly knocked the policeman over.

Martin the policeman was now all business, despite having known William for years. He put on his sternest voice. 'You shouldn't even be on that cart and, worse, you shouldn't be driving the children around in it, in your state. I'm ordering you to get them out of it right now.'

William couldn't have been more penitent. He hung his head, looking abject and shameful and so contrite you'd think he'd learned his lesson once and for all. The children in the cart stared wide-eyed at the constable, mouths hanging open, while that old cart horse with its hairy legs and swayback swished his tail as if telling everyone to get a move on, his dinner was waiting.

By now a small crowd had gathered, looking for some entertainment. William's kiddies were hanging out of the cart talking and laughing with some of their friends who'd come running out when William was stopped. There was an almighty ruckus when the youngest dropped his ball and nearly fell out himself when he tried to catch it as it went. Luckily, the older children knew enough of their father's habits to realize they were responsible for the little ones and so pulled him back before the whole thing turned into a complete disaster.

William ignored the fuss going on in and around the cart. He lifted his head and looked straight at the policeman. 'You're right, Martin.' Slowly, with as much dignity as he could muster in the alcoholic haze he was in, William climbed down from the cart. Leaving it right there on the main street in the middle of the town, he unhitched the harness. Then he took his children out of the cart one by one and hoisted them on to the patient horse. Before Martin even knew what he was up to, William jumped up on the horse behind them and trotted away out down the street, knowing his steady old horse could steer his way home blindfolded.

A loud cheer went up from the crowd, while Martin gaped, his mouth hanging open just like a kid. He was no more than a kid himself, to be honest, and not a match for

William, the wily bugger. The horse plodded on, and the crowd cheered again as the two older children, each holding tight to a younger one with one hand, waved the other triumphantly to their friends.

Martin, when he recovered his voice, shouted like all hell was breaking loose. 'Stop, William! Stop at once, d'you hear me?'

But William either didn't hear, or didn't wish to hear, for he kept that cart horse plodding on. The family smallholding was a fair way away, in a wooded hamlet tucked in a valley a good few miles from the town and, like the horse, William was keen for his dinner too. So all Martin could do was watch them go, getting madder and more frustrated by the minute. When hollering his head off didn't work, he blew on his whistle furiously, to no effect except to spur on the children – and William's drinking mates, who were also watching the fun – to cheer even more wildly as the horse disappeared around a bend and out of sight.

Next day, would you believe, William breezed into the town bold as a fox. He was sitting on his old horse as sprightly as can be, not an inch the worse for his drinking the day before. He was clear-eyed and cleanshaven and hopped off that horse like he was a lifelong teetotaller and a pillar of the community. Cocky as a rooster, he went up to his cart – still in the middle of the town – and hitched it up to bring it home.

At first, Martin, spotting him, couldn't believe his eyes. The cheek of the man, smiling and waving at the shopkeepers and folk out on the street as if he were the town mayor, instead of slinking back shamefaced, all full of apologies. The policeman ran over to give him a piece of his mind, but before he could speak William threw back his shoulders, lifted his chin and cried out, 'Constable Martin, I was hoping to find you. I do so thank you for your bit of advice yesterday.' He gave the policeman a huge grin. 'And now I'd like to give you a small token to say how grateful I am that we've got you here in our town looking after us.'

Once again, Martin was speechless. William wasn't much known for being a talker, and this was pretty much, coming from him. Before the policeman could gather his wits, William thrust a package wrapped in plain brown paper into his hand. It was wet and soggy, and Martin held it at arm's length with a look on his face like he was expecting something to leap out of the package and bite his fingers.

'Take it, it's for you,' William urged. 'A nice bit of trout, only caught this morning.'

The look on Martin's face was a wonderful sight to see as it changed from irritation and distaste to slow realization of what the package contained. He opened his mouth to say something then thought better and closed it again. He had a wife and three young ones under four to feed, and he not that old himself. Times were hard then, as I've said before. So he didn't ask who caught the fish, or where, or anything else about it. When he finally spoke it was just to say, 'Thank you, William. I sure do appreciate it.'

The two men shook hands. Only when they parted did Martin call out, casual like, to William, 'I take it you got those youngsters of yours home in one piece yesterday?'

William looked bemused that the man even had to ask. 'Why, certainly I did, and in time for dinner too.' He shook his head. Looking puzzled, he stared at Martin then said, 'Why are you asking?'

CHAPTER 4

Pixies and Cider

I THOUGHT ABOUT JULIE'S GRANDFATHER'S ANTICS OFF AND ON the rest of the afternoon, wondering what he'd have made of all the changes the last decades have brought. I do know one thing: for all his wild and reckless ways, he'd have been as furious as I was if he'd have seen those empty beer cans and whiskey bottles on Anstey Common. Litter was unheard of in those days, and even when we went poaching we packed away the wrappings from the sandwiches and pasties we'd brought with us and carted it back home with the fish we caught. Folk might not have had much, but they had their pride for certain things.

When I was up to Anstey Common next, still trying to get a photo of that darn cuckoo that kept hiding from me, I was heartened to see that there was no more rubbish strewn about, so maybe it was no more than a one-off thing. There was only the yellow gorse, clumps of withy trees and scrub oak here and there, that rough old mossy grass, and a couple of small may trees coming out in bloom at last. It looked just as it did every spring, and I said to myself, 'Thank the good Lord, some things never change.'

I said this to Julie that evening. She was in the garden looking at the leaves on the apple trees finally starting to come out, and about time too, as it was nearly May. 'It was probably the pixies, up on Anstey Common,' she said with a laugh. 'They're supposed to be responsible for all the mischief around here. Or they used to be, years back.'

I had to laugh too. There are so many stories and legends told about the West Country, but maybe the ones about the pixies are the ones that go back the farthest. Exmoor has its share of these stories, just like everywhere else, and like Julie said, pixies used to be blamed for a great deal of troublemaking. In the olden days, folk used to talk of being led astray by pixies. These were tiny people who sometimes wore green and had pointed ears. They were mischievous little people, but hard working as well. They used to help the countrypeople by working in the fields, so folk said, as long as they were left a bit of bread and cheese and cider in return. Sometimes they were known to give a hand with the housework – but other times, they could do just the opposite, mess up the house and make it untidy. You never knew where you were with those pixies!

Along with those mysterious little people, there was Jack O'Lantern, who used to roam around Exmoor, according to the old tales. This Jack was a naughty little fellow, appearing as a pale-blue light in the darkest nights, on marshy ground and churchyards. The eerie blue light was thought to be from his lantern and would entice people to wander into bogs and other places they shouldn't have. Of course, nowadays, you don't hear much about Jack O'Lantern, not since an explanation was found for the strange blue light. It turned out to be nothing more than gas burning slowly from decomposing animal or vegetable matter in the boggy ponds and marshland.

I've not heard any such explanation for pixies, but there are dozens, maybe hundreds, of pixie stories. Like the one about the tiny folk who used to do all the threshing at Withypool. The farmers there hardly had to work at all, so the story goes, for the pixies did it all for them!

Many good deeds were said to be done by the pixies, but there were also the other kind. Sometimes naughty ones would lead men into pubs, where they drank the night away. Now that's a great tale to tell the wife after a night on the razzle. 'I couldn't help it, m'dear, t'were the pixies led me there.' That story wouldn't work with my wife, let me tell you!

There's another tale about a place in the Barle Valley up on Exmoor called Cow Castle, or Ring Castle. It's an Iron Age fort on a low hill, built two or three thousand years ago. The story goes that, long ago, the good pixies were always at war with some nasty spirits so one day the queen of the pixies had this castle built. It wasn't just an ordinary castle, no way. You see, each stone and each bit of turf used to build this place was chock-full of the memory of someone's good deed, and of course this created such a powerful atmosphere that those evil spirits couldn't get a look-in.

Maybe all our houses should be built by our good deeds! What a world that would be, right?

There seems to have been a whole load of pixie activity around Dartmoor too, according to the legends. A woman living on the edge of the moor many years ago had a very beautiful garden, the prettiest in the whole county. She had every flower you could think of, but the best of all were her tulips. She had all colours, red and yellow and some deep purple ones too.

Now, the pixies loved this woman's garden. When it started to get dark, they'd bring their pixie babies there to sing them to sleep. The scent of those tulips was so intoxicating they were like a drug, giving the little ones the sweetest sleep ever. And while the babies slept, the grown-up pixies danced all night, until they vanished in the morning, leaving no more than a ring of trampled grass where they'd danced.

The pixies got to love these tulips so much that they cast a spell on them, making them last longer than ordinary flowers, and smell even sweeter. The old woman was happy about this, as you can imagine. Her garden was better than ever! She never let anyone pick a single one of her flowers, but left it for the village folk to visit and admire, and for the pixies to dance in it at night.

This went on for years, until the woman eventually died. A niece or nephew or some such relative inherited her cottage, but this person wasn't too keen on flowers and planted other odds and sods, taking out the flowers. Where the tulips had been, they planted parsley.

Oh my, did this make those pixies furious! They cast another spell on the garden, only this time it wasn't such a nice one. The parsley withered, and nothing else grew in that garden ever again.

But the pixies never forgot their friend. Her grave was always green and covered with flowers, all the work of those little creatures. And in the springtime, for years, you could hear sweet music coming from her burial place, and the scent of fresh flowers stayed there day and night.

There are also many stories of strange pixie births, some going back two or three centuries. Another Dartmoor story is about the midwife who was called from her home in the middle of the night by a strange man on a black horse saying his wife was about to have a baby and she must go with him at once. The midwife was scared out of her wits, as the man seemed odd to her, hardly speaking, gruff like. But she felt compelled to go and got up behind him on his horse.

They travelled through the night up to the middle of the moor, skirting the boggy bits that the horse seemed to know instinctively. When they finally got to the man's cottage, it was clean and warm and cosy, which made the midwife feel heaps better.

The wife, an ordinary young woman, gave birth to twins. After she'd rested a bit, she took out a small glass jar of a strange ointment she'd had under her pillow and asked the midwife to rub some in the twins' eyes. When the midwife protested that it didn't sound like such a good idea, the mother got so agitated that the other woman did as she asked. But the midwife also put a bit in her own eyes, curious to know what the stuff was.

The minute she did it, the woman and babies in front of her changed before her eyes. The mother was a beautiful pixie woman and her twins were so tiny you could hold them both in one hand. They were covered with a fine silvery cloth, thin and delicate as a spider's web. Terrified, the midwife ran out of the house, where the man was standing waiting with his horse. She jumped on the back again and he took her home without a word.

For years after that, the midwife and her family tried to find that cottage on the moor, but never could. Some say it still exists there on deepest Dartmoor, through having seen lights on foggy nights shining through the windows of a cottage that disappears in daylight.

Pixies are very good at returning favours, I hear. They never forget it if someone helps them out in any way. Like the man who rescued a pixie from a bog up on Dartmoor. This poor little creature had slipped into a bog and was going under fast, struggling to get out of the mud that was sucking him down. A young fellow heard the pixie's cries and threw a thin bit of rope out to him, then pulled the tiny person to safety.

As a reward, the pixie gave the man a ring. He didn't want to take it, being as he was a very kind person and didn't want a reward for saving someone's life. But the pixie insisted, saying that the ring was magic and would make him invisible whenever he was in danger. The bloke wasn't that impressed, saying that he didn't really have a need for being invisible, thank you. But then the pixie told him that the ring also would give him the power to see through fog and mist. Now *that* interested this young man, for he knew what an advantage that would be when walking or riding on the moor.

It's a good job he took that ring, let me tell you. Because up on the part of the moor where he liked to walk, there lived a witch called Vixana. She wasn't a very nice witch, for sure. Her favourite pastime was to bring down a thick fog on the moor when people were travelling on it. Now, anyone who has been on any of the West Country moors when a heavy mist comes down knows how dangerous it is. You can lose your sense of direction in minutes. This is what used to happen to people when that witch made a spell to bring down the fog. They'd get completely confused and start wandering about off the paths and high ground, and fall right into a bog!

Well, what happened was this. The young chap with the magic pixie ring was travelling across the moor when spiteful Vixana saw him and conjured up the fog. But instead of falling into the bog, the man seemed to disappear. His ring had made him invisible, you see. Not only was he invisible, but he also could see the witch through the mist. He snuck up on her from behind and pushed her off the high rocky tor, where she fell into a deep black bog. So that was the end of Vixana, but you can still see the outcrop of rocks where she used to hang out. Vixen Tor, it's called. And you can walk around it and over it quite safely now without worrying about the witch, thanks to the pixie and his magic ring.

Like many of us in the West Country, the pixies are known to like their cider. Leaving a glass or two out for them always encourages the little folk to concentrate on doing good deeds rather than mischievous ones. In some places long ago, when they made cider, they left a few apples on the tree for the pixies. And when the brew was all done and ready to drink, some of it was poured on the apple tree for the pixies to have a taste of it themselves.

Talking about apple trees makes me think of a farmer near Anstey who used to make cider. This man, called Jim, had a few acres that he didn't do much with but one thing he did have was apple trees. He had a small orchard, just over an acre of trees, which gave a good crop of cider apples every year.

Jim's father had been making cider for years, and Jim had taken it over in a big way. He had all the equipment to make a strong homebrew, which he did with his own apples every year. It was his biggest source of income, selling his cider to neighbours and friends and anyone else who found out about Jim's cider through word of mouth. This was fifty, sixty years ago, mind. Things were done different then, for sure, and many a law-abiding citizen turned a blind eye to the making and selling of illegal cider, especially if it was good stuff and they could get it cheap.

Folk who had heard of Jim's homebrew but didn't know how to go about buying it found out somehow. You had to drive up to Jim's ramshackle old farmhouse with its rotting window frames, holey thatched roof and rough lane, and go around through a brambly bit of garden to get to the back door. There was a kind of porch-type thing full of Jim's boots and tools and suchlike, and a shelf with a half-dead spider plant on it. If you wanted a bottle of cider you put the money – I've forgotten now how much it was, if I ever knew, as I was only a young lad – on the shelf under the spider plant, and rang an old-fashioned brass horse bell hanging there. Then you had to dis-appear for a few minutes, go out in front of the house and admire the trees or some such thing. When you got back, the money would be gone, but there would be a full bottle of cider on that shelf.

No one ever saw Jim exchange money for cider, ever, so he could swear on the Bible if he had to. It was a good system. Jim could see a car or person coming up his rough track from wherever he was on the land and be out of sight before they got there. On the rare days when Jim was at market or at the pub, that back door would be shut and the customer would know to come another time. But even Jim's best mates had to go through the same routine if they wanted to buy a bottle of his homebrew. No magistrate could ever accuse Jim of selling cider, no way. As he said, 'If folk want to give me a few bob now and again, what's it to anyone? And what's the law against giving a bottle of cider to a friend, every so often? None as far as I can ruddy well see.'

Not everyone thought the same. Our local constable, who must have known about Jim's business but turned a blind eye, had some kind of illness that laid him up for about six months, so another police officer was brought in to replace him. Now this fellow was a good man I'm sure, but he didn't know the ways of the countryside, being from Taunton or Exeter or some such city. He got wind of Jim's business and decided to put a stop to it. He'd hung around the local pubs talking to the customers so had a fair idea what to do. Sure enough, Jim comes out with his bottle of homebrew, takes the cash and, at this moment, the policeman shouts, 'Ha, caught you! You're under arrest for selling illegal alcohol.'

Jim didn't bat an eyelid. 'You got nothing on me, sir,' he said, polite as can be. 'I came out thinking I had visitors, wanting to offer them a bit of cider, and I was right, there you are!'

'Don't give me that. You took my money, sure enough.'

Jim looked perplexed. 'Oh, this? Is this yours?' He handed the man back his cash. 'I didn't take it, sir, it was just lying there on my property so I did what any man would do, picked it up. But if it's yours, why, fine. Now why don't you try some of this fine cider, Constable, considering you've come all the way out here? Be my guest!'

Would you believe, the policeman did just that. The story goes that he tasted it at first for evidence, to make sure it was truly cider – he didn't want to be made a fool of – but the stuff was so tasty, and so strong, that he and Jim had a right old night and parted best of friends. When that policeman went back to Taunton, Jim's business boomed. Word of mouth is a great thing for sales, and Jim's special homebrew, and the low price he charged, made it worth driving for a long way.

I remember Jim had his own pixie story he'd heard up near Exeter way. Apparently, around that area many years back there was a man and his wife that did a pixie a favour. Now, no one knows what that favour was, but the pixie never forgot it. Those pixies, they could be mean and have their revenge if folk thwarted them in any way, but as we know, they sure as hell remembered those who were kindly towards them.

So these two people near Exeter were rewarded by the pixies for whatever favour they'd done the little folk, and the reward was a good one. They cast a spell so that the barrel of cider the couple kept in their cellar never ran dry. Can you imagine it? A cider barrel that always stayed full, no matter how many pints you pulled from it!

This enchanted barrel of cider stayed in the family for

years and years. Generations of the family drank from that never-ending keg until one day a nosy servant went down to draw a jug from the barrel. Curious about the story, she took off the lid, which had never been removed, to peer inside. What a shock she got when she saw there was nothing there, just a dry old barrel full of cobwebs. It frightened her to death, having just poured a cup from the tap. She slammed the lid down in a fright and turned the tap on again, but no cider came out. And it never did again. Those pixies were so indignant that they took away the spell. That magic barrel was now nothing but an ordinary empty cider keg.

Touchy creatures, pixies! You got to be careful what you do and say around them!

CHAPTER 5

The Flying Fish of Exmoor

THINKING ABOUT SOME OF THESE STORIES FROM LONG AGO, I got to thinking about Tony, one of my best mates for many years. He's passed on now, sudden like, only a few years ago, still in his early sixties. He was quite a character and we did many things together. He never married but lived alone out at his place in Twichen, not far from me, where he died. I miss him a lot, but thinking of our times still gives me a warm feeling, puts a smile on my face. Driving past the River Bray the other day, I stopped the truck to lean over the old stone bridge and watch the water rushing over the rocks, remembering all the times I used to poach salmon in this very spot.

The river was running fast. The beech trees along the bank were coming out in new leaf and the primroses were making a mass of colour everywhere. There I was, a man of seventy-one now, leaning over that bridge and thinking about being in this same spot over fifty years ago. God knows, it's hard to believe it was that long ago that my mate Tony and me went poaching under this same bridge.

It was late autumn but the day was like this one, sunny and warm. Now, as I've said before, in those days I poached fish, and rabbit and even deer, to get a bit of meat on the table, for life was hard and, without it, our diet would've been pretty limited, let me tell you. Now, of course, I couldn't kill anything – I stalk the wild animals on Exmoor to shoot them with a camera, not a gun, but in those old days poaching was a way of life. An old, honourable way of life, if you look at it one way, as poaching on Exmoor is an ancient tradition that goes back to medieval times. The red deer is the largest surviving native animal in this country and the Exmoor herd is thought to be the oldest of these herds. There are about a couple of thousand left now but there were many more once. The place was full of deer and many of the titled people of England liked to hunt there.

So Exmoor always has attracted hunters – and where there are hunters, you can bet there are poachers. As I said, my mates and I were following a long tradition!

That day on the river, I'd come with my mate Tony to see if we could catch a salmon for our dinner, or even to sell for some extra income. Now, another mate, Brian, was supposed to be joining us. I'd known Brian for even longer than Tony, as he'd been in school with Julie. It was Sunday afternoon, and Tony and I had put away a few ciders before getting to the work at hand, so we were pretty relaxed and easy. It was one of those golden days with a hazy sun and still plenty of light to spot the fish. 'Only there's plenty of light to spot us, Tony,' I said, 'which won't do at all, so we best be careful.'

You see, normally, there wouldn't have been much activity over old Bray Bridge, but as it was a Sunday, there were folk about every now and again, walking over the bridge on the way to evening service at the chapel.

So we had to be a bit extra careful. I'd found a good spot under the narrow bridge where I couldn't be seen from the road above. It was a perfect place, a couple of beech trees on the riverbed, the leaves a bright yellow, not wanting to give in to winter any more than the rest of us. The sun, though low in the sky, was still pumping out a bit of warmth, despite the season.

'This looks good,' I said, getting out my fishing gear. There was another bottle of cider for each of us, a bag to hide the fish in, and my dung pick, which was a kind of pitchfork with four prongs.

'Looks good to me too, Johnny.' Tony leaned back against one of the beech trees. 'Could sit here all day, I could, watching the river, drinking the cider.'

'Okay, Tony, but keep your bledy eyes open for fish,' I told him with a grin, as his eyelids were drooping down like he was planning to spend the next hour or two snoozing.

I was standing, looking down over the water, hoping there was something good down there, worth either a few good meals for us or to make a bit of cash to buy a few good meals. I was holding my dung fork; it felt good in my hand. I'd had it a long time, but it was still sharp, still reliable. We were old friends, me and that dung pick.

Tony was awake but still leaning against the tree like he hadn't a care in the world, drinking his cider and talking away. 'There's nothing like it, Johnny, is there, this fishing business. A man's his own boss, the whole outdoors is where he works, yes indeed, what a life, I could stay here all day, Johnny, I really could.' I looked around at him as his voice tailed off, and sure enough he was drifting off to sleep again.

'Hey, Tony,' I said, 'maybe you should get up on the bridge now.' I was ready to go, looking for a big one, and we'd agreed it'd be Tony's job to be lookout. You never knew when some suspicious officer of the law might appear, or someone who thought he owned this part of the river. As Tony finished his cider, I said, 'Now, any person or car that don't look right, mate, you start cawing like a bledy crow, and me and my dung pick will be off and away in seconds. You get that?'

Tony nodded.

I went on, 'When I catch a fish, I'm gonna try and throw it right up on to the bridge and it'll be your job to get it and hide it quick, right?'

'Right, Johnny. Quick as lightning I'll be.'

Now, like I said, our mate Brian was supposed to be up

on that bridge too, but he'd been held up somewhere so Tony had to be bloody vigilant. Brian's job was to distract any of the churchgoers who weren't in a hurry, who thought it might be a fine idea to stop a while, look over the bridge to see if anything was going on down there. Brian knew everyone in the whole entire village, and he'd get them talking about something else until they forgot they'd intended to look down at the river before moving on.

Tony still hadn't budged. He was having a high old time, enjoying the sunshine on that river bank. So I said again, 'C'mon, mate, you'd better get up on that bridge, especially as Brian's not here yet.'

'Right you are, Johnny. Right you are, mate. It's time we got some fish, Johnny, right?'

'Right, Tony.'

'Yep, grand day for it. Not a breath of wind, like. Nothing like it, day like today, out on the river.'

Now Tony was a great bloke, my best mate, but by hell he was a talker. He went on and on, not moving a sodding inch but not stopping the gabbing. Now I'm a talker too, but there's a time and place for talking and a time and place for fishing. I knew he'd go on like that until it was too bloody dark to see the fish, so I had to put it to him bluntly. 'Now see here, Tony, me mate,' I said, looking straight at him. 'You got to stop talking, all right? You got to stop bledy yapping, get up on that bledy bridge, and let's get us some fish.'

The thing I loved about Tony was that he never got

offended when you talked straight to him. He nodded and scurried up to the bridge, still jabbering away about how great it was to go fishing on a sunny river bank with a few ciders in your belly. I have to say it was a relief when he was out of hearing, not that I minded his yapping. It's just that talking's no good when you're doing some serious fishing.

So now Tony was in place, ready and waiting. I got myself settled on a slab of rock where the water formed a nice, still pool. It was a good place for salmon this time of year, spawning time. They'd lie there motionless for ages, not too deep down, and you could see their dark shapes under the water, with that flash of silver underneath as they swam away.

I stood just as motionless as those salmon at the river's edge, while Tony stood on the edge of the bridge, ready to make his crow call of warning if any trouble seemed to be coming our way. And ready, too, to grab hold of a fish as soon as I caught one and tossed it up on the bridge for him to catch and hide.

The sun was warm on my face and a bit of a breeze swished above me in the yellow-leafed trees, but all the time I was focused on that river, watching that water for a fish. Once or twice I thought I spotted one and lifted my arm high, dung pick tight in my hand, my whole body tensed with readiness for the throw.

But they were only shadows, or branches submerged in water slowly drifting past. No salmon. Not for ages.

Finally, the real thing came along, and once again my

body tensed, but this one was too far away, out of reach. Years of experience had taught me not to strike too soon, to be patient, wait until I was sure. I stood there willing that fish to come a little closer. C'mon, you bugger, just a bit, lemme get at you . . . But it was no use. It swam away, completely out of reach.

But I wasn't too worried. In those days there were plenty more where that one came from and, sure enough, I was in luck. Right away, another salmon drifted within striking distance. I lifted my pick. He was a big'un, about 10 or 12 pounds for sure. I stabbed him all right but that was only the beginning. Because the fork had no barbs to stop the fish from falling off, I had to be faster than lightning lifting him straight up right out of the water, to stop him from falling off the prongs. Even holding the fork sideways would have lost him.

I struggled with all my strength to hold him upright as he wiggled on the dung pick. 'Bledy fish,' I shouted over and over, and lots of other swear words and cursing as well, believe me. I hoped to hell Brian had arrived and was helping Tony keep those chapel people away.

'He's getting away, the bugger,' I hollered as water flew everywhere and the fish thrashed and fought on my pick. I thought my wrists would break as the pole was slippery with water and turning in my hands. If I didn't hold it fast, the prongs would turn downwards again and the fish would slide back into the water and be out of sight before I had another chance at it.

He gave me a good fight. I heard Tony shouting, 'You

all right there, Johnny?' but I was swearing so hard I couldn't answer. I was drenched in water and sweat, trying to keep the pick upright, struggling to hold that wet pole straight, trying to keep my balance and not fall into the river myself. The smooth rock I was standing on was wet and slippery and I had to move around to hold on to that fish.

My arms and wrists were tiring fast by then and I knew one of us would have to win or lose soon. So I gave a final heave and threw him up high, high over the river, and he flew off the fork and into the air and over the bridge just like he was supposed to do. I caught that fish, I thought, as I panted and swore with the exertion, the river water streaming off me in buckets.

When I could breathe near enough to normal again, I called out to Tony to see if he'd got the fish. He didn't answer. It was dead quiet up on that bridge. So that was good – none of the churchgoers had walked across when the fish flew over. It was a big one too. I grinned when I thought of the expression on Tony's face when the bloody big salmon sailed over his head and landed near him with a bang.

But there was still no sound coming from up there. No one hollering down that they got the fish and had hid it out of sight. In fact, there was no sound of talking even. I knew Brian had finally got there – he'd shouted down to me while I was struggling with the fish – so why weren't he and Tony yapping? It wasn't like my mates to be quiet!

'Oh bledy hell,' I said aloud, a terrible thought coming to me. 'I hope it didn't hit Brian or Tony.'

Oh Lord, I thought, a fish that size could kill a man.

So I was that relieved when I saw Brian's face leaning over the wall of the bridge, and next to him Tony's. I shouted up, 'Did you get the salmon?'

Tony shook his head. 'It's out of sight, Johnny, long gone. I mean, really and truly gone.'

'What d'you mean?'

Tony was still shaking his head, and now Brian was too. They looked like a couple of dying fish themselves, faces all gloomy and heads waving back and forth like they were caught in a current.

'I can't believe it, Johnny,' Tony said. 'Just like that, gone. I'd never have believed it if I hadn't seen it with my own eyes, Johnny. Never.'

'Yep, me too,' Brian said. 'Never have believed it if I hadn't seen it with my own two eyes.'

'Naw, nor me, Johnny. Chances are one in a million of that happening.' Tony was scratching his head, looking perplexed as hell.

'Yep, one in a million,' Brian repeated, like a damn parrot.

Tony said, 'Shame, though. Looked like a big 'un, that fish.'

'Tony!' I shouted up. 'Will you stop talking? Both of you! Stop talking and tell me what the hell happened to my fish. What d'you mean, it's gone? It's on that bloody bridge somewhere. Where the hell else could it be?'

Brian and Tony exchanged looks. Tony said, 'Well, it was heading towards South Molton way, might even be there by now. If that's where it was going.'

Well, I finally got the story out of those two. That fish I caught flew right over the bridge just as an open-top sports car was driving by, and would you believe, it landed smack in the back, while Brian and Tony stared in astonishment.

'Driver didn't even stop,' Brian said. 'Couldn't have heard the bump as the fish fell in. Had the car radio blaring away so loud the folks up at chapel would've heard it. No way he'd notice another thump or two.'

Tony nodded. 'It was going like a bat out of hell.'

'What? The fish or the sports car?'

'Both,' they said in unison.

It was a daft question, and I must've been in shock to have asked it. I shook my head. So did the others. We looked a right bunch of idiots, our dinner snatched right out of our hands like that. Tony said, 'The driver's gonna get a right shock when he sees that big salmon in the back of his vehicle.'

'Lucky sod,' Brian said.

'Unlucky us,' I muttered.

Tony said, 'You should have seen it, Johnny. Whizzing through the air like a flying fish. That sports car speeding over the bridge, music blaring. You couldn't of timed it better.' He was grinning now.

'Naw,' Brian said. 'Couldn't of timed it better.'

For the first time since I'd known him, Tony couldn't

say another word. He and Brian were laughing like hell and, before long, I was laughing too, though it damn well hurt to lose that fish.

But what can you do? Lose some, win some.

We didn't get a fish dinner that night but we had a fine story to tell in the pub.

And we never did find out whose sports car that was, and where my fish ended up that day.

But you know something? The people in that car are going to be telling that story to this day, and so are their children and grandchildren. They wouldn't have had a clue where that beautiful salmon came from, so they would have speculated. And other folk would too, and more would be added to it, and it would get twisted around, until one day you'll hear the legend of the Flying Fish of Exmoor. Or maybe it'll be the Ghost Fish of Exmoor, or maybe even the fish will have turned into the Flying Mermaid.

Whatever you hear, remember you heard it first from Johnny Kingdom!

CHAPTER 6

The Hairy Hand

TONY AND I WERE SO ALIKE, MAYBE THAT'S WHY WE GOT ON SO well. We were both tearaways when we were young, and then later we both got interested in wildlife. No one outside my family was as pleased for me as Tony when my wildlife photography started to get noticed. I remember how excited he was when I got my first films of the otters, on the Torridge River. I'd never filmed the creatures before and I got some great shots, some of two otter cubs playing. The otter is an amazing animal. It's a large carnivorous mammal, living mainly on fish and eels. It roams all over the place, moving through wetlands in an area of about 40km. The otter builds its holts along the rivers, streams and ponds along his way. Some are in riverside tree roots, or at the edge of marshes, or in tall vegetation.

When I had the pond dug on our land to attract the wildlife, I had an island built up in the middle, with all the timbers and suchlike put there to make a holt. I hope to attract otters there one day, along the small stream that leads into the pond. There's a wonderful old birch tree that was gently uprooted and put on the island. Oh my, what a job that was! It was all captured on film for the BBC series I did. We managed to save that birch tree, and it's still there, in the middle of the island.

Julie said now, as we were sat there talking about these old times, 'You miss Tony still, don't you, Johnny.' It wasn't a question but a true statement of my feelings. Nearly three years ago now that Tony died, and I think of him every day. My wife knows me well, knows how deep my affection is for all the old friends I knew then and know now.

'The trouble with remembering these old stories,' I said, 'is that it saddens a person, thinking of all those wonderful folk gone.'

Julie nodded. But then she said, 'But Johnny, think of those still left. Old friends have passed away, but look at all the new ones you've found. And our parents and many of our old relations have gone, but we've got our two sons, and our two lovely granddaughters, Roxie and Louise.'

Julie was right, of course. Change is tough sometimes, but if one generation didn't pass away, it'd be too crowded for the next one to be born.

As usual, my wife managed to cheer me up. I was a lucky man.

*

We had a thick mist creep over Exmoor the other night, and it lasted well into the next day. It seemed to follow me over to Dartmoor, where I had to go to give a talk. When I left, one of the organizers said to me, with a laugh, 'Don't let the hairy hands get hold of you on the way home!'

I hadn't a clue what she was on about. She explained, 'It's an old legend from Dartmoor – you must have heard the story.'

'Oh aye,' I said. 'We've got plenty of those up on Exmoor, but what's your version, then? I've heard tell about this Hairy Hand, so tell me some more.'

'I was told this when I first moved to Devon, some thirty years ago,' she said. 'In fact, many people told me the same story. There's a road along Dartmoor where it's dangerous to drive across, especially at night. Two huge, strong, severed hands suddenly appear out of nowhere and grab the steering wheel, forcing the car off the road. Motorcyclists are especially vulnerable to the hand. Cyclists, too, and even horses and carts, long ago. There were many accidents along that road, in the early 1900s especially, and people told of these terrible hands. Sometimes it was nothing more than an evil presence in the car that made them swerve and crash.'

'That's bloody bad enough,' I said.

But there was plenty more. This road is in the middle of Dartmoor, and is a pretty lonely one. The first instance of these supernatural hands happened in 1921, and the story's been told again and again. A man who worked at Dartmoor prison had a bad crash on this road. He was riding along on a dark night with his two kiddies in the sidecar when all of a sudden they heard their father screaming and shouting at someone to get off the bike, let go of the handles. They were terrified, seeing their dad struggling to keep control but having a bad time, as if someone was trying to wrest the handlebars away from him. The motorbike crashed and, luckily, the two children jumped free, but the man was killed.

Those kids swore that something was pulling the bike out of control, but they saw nothing, only the crazy movements of the handlebars and their father trying to push something away and hold on to the steering mechanism at the same time.

The odd thing was that the same thing happened again to another motorcyclist, not all that long afterwards, and on the same road. This time there was a passenger in the sidecar who swore he saw something trying to grab the handlebars. It was a large hairy hand that actually took hold of the bars and, using superhuman force, upset the bike.

Campers sometimes have seen it too. There's a story from back in 1924 about a couple in a caravan not far from that spooky place. The woman woke up suddenly, her heart racing, feeling that something evil was lurking about, ready to do harm to her and her husband. It was a moonlit night, and she sat up in her bunk bed, too frightened to move. She was facing the caravan window and, there in front of her, she saw the hand. It was big and rough and ghostly looking and it filled the whole window. The woman, in a state of terror, made the sign of the cross, and the hand vanished.

Now this road is between Postbridge and Two Bridges, not far from Dartmoor prison, and later on that day I had to go along it, coming from Moretonhampstead. I have to admit, with the eerie mist haunting those granite tors of the moor, I wouldn't have been surprised to see those hands come out! Lucky for me, whoever those nasty hands belong to, they stayed in their pockets that day and I made it safely home.

There are so many haunted places on Dartmoor, but this same woman told me a story I hadn't heard before, about a place called Lydford. There's the remains of a castle there on a hill, where a black phantom pig has been seen snuffling and snorting in amongst the ruins. Folk say he's the ghost of the terrible hanging judge, Judge Jeffreys, who was responsible for putting many people to death at that castle. This was in the 1600s, I do believe. At the end of the village of Lydford is a grassy mound known as Gallows Hill, and many say they've heard moaning and wailing coming from there. All those poor sods that Judge Jeffreys condemned to death.

Not far from the village is Lydford Gorge, a spectacular steep granite ravine with the River Lyd running through it. A famous haunting there is done by a woman who was probably drowned or slashed to death by the rocks in the gorge, for she's seen by many, staring into a pool of water called Kit's Steps. She's called the Red Lady, because she always has a red kerchief or shawl on her.

You can see why Dartmoor is home to all these ghost stories. It's a lot more barren than Exmoor, more rocky, and has magnificent tors of granite, while Exmoor is gentler, with its wooded valleys and hidden combes. Both are splendid in their own way, but on a day like today, with that fog stretching out in front of me, I'd say Dartmoor is the most mysterious. But maybe that's because I know Exmoor better. It's been my home for over seventy years, after all, and you sure as hell get to know a place in that long time!

Another moor with many legends is Bodmin Moor, down in Cornwall. Many people have heard of Jamaica Inn, which stands in the middle of the moor and has many spooky tales told about it. It's been haunted by many ghosts, and people who have stayed there have seen and heard many strange things. For years, different landlords and managers have heard footsteps tramping up and down a passageway to the bar. The story is that they're the footsteps of a man who died before finishing his drink and spends eternity going back for it again and again. Other landlords heard voices speaking in a strange language. Later, they thought it might have been Cornish. People say they've heard the clatter of hooves in the middle of the night when no horses were anywhere near the place.

There was a murder at the inn many years ago. A stranger to Bodmin Moor came in one night and ordered a tankard of ale. He was enjoying his drink in a relaxed manner when someone – no one ever found out who it was – called to him to come outside for a minute. He left his beer half finished and went out. That was the last time he was seen alive. The next day his body was found up in the most desolate part of the moor you can imagine. He was thought to have been murdered, but no one ever found out who did it. Was it the person who called him out? Or someone else? The mystery is still unsolved.

Some folks say that it's the ghost of this man that walks up and down the passageway, to finish his drink. Not only that but, in the early 1900s, many people saw a strange man sitting motionless on the wall outside the inn. He never moved, nor did he speak, even when people greeted him. The odd thing was that the man looked exactly like the bloke who was murdered!

There are people who swear that the man sitting on the wall was the ghost of the murdered man. Who knows? There are so many strange things said to happen on all the moors that some of them must be true, don't you think?

CHAPTER 7

Magic Trees and Ravens

IT WAS NEARLY MAY, BUT SPRING WAS LATE. UP ON THE HIGHER moor, the oak wasn't showing any leaves yet, though the ash trees were greening up. I guess everyone in England knows the old saying:

> When the oak is out before the ash,
> We shall only have a splash.
> But if the ash is out before the oak,
> We shall have a summer soak.

I was thinking, if that old saying is true, I'll have some wet safaris this summer. That's what I do now, along with taking my photographs, and doing filming for the BBC. In the spring and summer months, and early autumn, I take four people at a time in my jeep and show them Exmoor, all the local beauty spots like Tarr Steps and Landacre Bridge, to name but a few. We go across the high moor and try to spot the red deer and other wildlife. I try to get across to folk my feelings about Exmoor, how precious it is, how wonderful.

It's far better for people if the sun is shining, but we go out in all weathers and, I have to say, most of my visitors are good-natured and don't let a spot of rain bother them. Though a summer splash would be better than a summer soak, that's for sure!

I had a chuckle when I thought of the other version of this old saying, one we locals used to chant:

> When the oak is out before the ash,
> Fills the farmers' pockets full of cash.
> But if the ash is out before the oak,
> Lord have mercy on us poor folk!

That got Julie and me giggling later, thinking about some of the old sayings. Julie said, '"When the days begin to lengthen/ Then the cold begins to strengthen."'

'Too bledy true,' I said. The days were truly getting longer and longer, but the nights were still frosty and there was a sneaky breeze. Which reminded me: 'When the wind blows hard from the east / 'Tis neither good for man nor beast.'

'I got another good one,' I went on. '"A whistling woman and a crowing hen, ain't no good to God nor men."'

'What about a whistling man?' Julie asked, laughing.

'That's different.' I started whistling as I left the kitchen. She rolled her eyes at me but had a smile on her face.

People really did believe in those old sayings, and some do now still. Farmers worried if the sun didn't shine on Christmas Day, New Year's Day and Old Christmas Day, which is 6 January. It meant a good crop of apples if the sun shone those three days; if not, a disastrous crop.

Talking of Christmas, here's a story about a famous West Country saint and the very first Christmas tree. Now, St Boniface was born a long time ago, way back in the seventh century, in a town in Devon called Crediton. When he was older he was sent to Germany as a missionary, to convert the pagans there to Christianity.

This St Boniface became the patron saint of brewers, and I wonder if that was why he was sent to beer-loving Germany: because he liked a pint every now and again! Who knows? The fact is, he worked very hard in Germany and set up many Christian churches and even became an archbishop there.

One day, he found himself in Bavaria, where he was working hard trying to tell people about Christianity. The story goes that at the winter solstice, he came across a group of pagans worshipping an old oak tree. Well, to St Boniface, this was not a pretty sight. He felt they were being blasphemous. He was so upset and horrified by this that he grabbed the nearest axe and chopped down that oak tree. He was a man of action, that saint, and he looked like a whirlwind coming into that group and hacking down the tree.

The pagans must have been a bit put out, this man tearing into their sacred tree like a madman, but apparently some of them listened to him when he said it was God not him who'd chopped down the tree, and this was just one example of God's power. According to the legends, some of them were converted right on the spot, though no doubt others went home a bit cross about the whole thing.

But then something amazing happened. A beautiful fir tree grew up suddenly on the spot where the oak tree was felled. St Boniface said that the evergreen was a symbol of God's love, which lasted for ever and ever, just like the green of the conifers. By the next year, all the pagans in Bavaria had converted to Christianity and, around the time of the winter solstice, which they now called Christmas, they put decorations on that fir tree in celebration, making it the very first Christmas tree ever.

Anyway, back to this time of year, springtime, which reminds me of the tramps we used to get in the villages and all around Exmoor. Though they were round and about all year long, it seemed springtime brought most of them. The warmer weather got them on the move again, after they had hunkered down during the coldest months.

There was a man called Dicky Slader who used to go around peddling second-hand tools from his cart. He came around our way twice every year, in spring, and then again in autumn. His wagon was pulled by an old brown cart horse with legs as sturdy as Dicky's from walking up and down the Exmoor hills. The horse had a wispy beard too, same as Dicky, though I don't think either of them was that old.

Dicky looked like a tramp most of the time, with torn clothes and his beard adorned with the odd bit of leaf or twig. But later in the year, at harvest time, he'd spruce himself up, clean as a whistle in his dressing-up clothes, and attend harvest teas at the village churches.

One day, he went to St Mary's Church in Molland. It's a fine church, very old, with a flagstone floor that makes it seem as if the church is sloping. It probably is, what with the age of it and the fact that it's on a hill. Perched in the middle of the small village, it's got views all around of green fields, woodland and moorland.

The church was rebuilt, so I've been told, sometime in the 1700s, but its font goes back years, to the twelfth century, I believe. It's got a good old feel to it still, with the old-fashioned box pews still there and in good shape. When my mates and I were young, we loved to go to the church in Molland with our girlfriends. The vicar couldn't see what we were up to with those wooden boxes for pews hiding all kinds of innocent mischief.

It's a very pretty village, Molland, with the pub and church, and now a place where you can get a good cup of tea and some cakes as well. Years ago, they used to have grand harvest teas there, and maybe they still do. This story about Dicky the pedlar happened a long time ago, mind, so I wouldn't know about the harvest teas now.

Anyhow, there Dicky was, up on his horse and pulling his cart, himself all spruced up for a change. I suspect the road there looked much the same as it does now, passing through bits of the moor with the heather all out at that time of year, and the gorse flowers a bright yellow. The beech trees along the way would have been turning the same colour and the other leaves would have started reddening and turning bronze and brown.

Dicky tethered his horse and walked up the incline to the church hall, where he helped himself to a plateful of home-made scones with good old-fashioned cream, thick as can be, with dollops of strawberry jam. Along with that he had a slab of fruitcake and a pile of sandwiches. You got a lot for your money, in those days, and all the proceeds went into the church funds.

As Dicky was eating, Farmer Huxtable came by. He greeted the tramp cordially, for Dicky was well known and well liked. The farmer said, 'Don't worry about paying for your tea. I'll do that.'

Dicky thanked him and helped himself to more scones and cake. After a while, another farmer came in. 'Hello there, Dicky, good to see you,' said the second farmer. 'Oh, and don't worry about paying for your tea, I'll buy it for you.'

Dicky replied, 'Thanks, mister, but that's all right, Farmer Huxtable is paying for this one. But next week I'll be at Heasley Mill for their harvest tea, so you can pay for that one.'

And the farmer did, too. At the next place, someone else offered to pay, and Dicky said, 'Well now, this tea is paid for, sir, but next week I'll be in Hawkridge, as I'm sure they will be doing a fine tea, thank you very much, and I'd appreciate it if you could pay for that one.' The person always did.

Dicky had a fine old time, going from church to church every autumn, filling up on all those wonderful home-made teas. He always managed to get someone else to pay, too, but nobody minded. Dicky was always polite and well mannered, and folk appreciated that. The churches were important in those long-ago days, not just for worship but to gather the villagers into a community as well. There are dozens of old stone churches tucked away in deep wooded combes on Exmoor, or up on the high moor on the crest of hills, or stuck squat in the middle of a tiny village the world seems to have forgotten about the last fifty years. I was up around Doone Valley the other day, passing Oare Church. Loads of visitors go there now, to visit the church made famous by R. D. Blackmore when he wrote the book *Lorna Doone*. It's still unspoiled though, the church and the river and the deep cleave of the valley. As I was passing by I heard the bells of the church begin to toll for a funeral being held that day. One of the locals had died, a man well past ninety, so there were cars parked for miles around and people standing outside listening to the service.

The church bells gladdened my heart, for they reminded me of the bells of all the village churches when

I was a very young boy. There were no phones then and so the bells were used to pass information on. When someone in the parish passed away, the church bell would ring three tolls for a man and two for a woman. Then a person's age was tolled, with everyone standing still, respectful like, and counting silently.

When someone died in the parish, everyone had to get themselves ready in good time for the funeral. If the men didn't have a dark suit, they'd go to the tailor to be measured, and it would be ready in five days. The men wore bowler hats. The women wore black for a year or, if they didn't have black clothes, they wore a black armband on their coats. Cards rimmed with black were sent for the funeral. It was all very formal, whether you were a rich landowner or a poor poacher and gravedigger. The communities were close knit in those days, and everyone went to the funeral.

There's a story told in High Bray about the missing gravedigger at one of the funerals at a nearby village. No one could find him, even though they searched high and low all around the church, up in the choir loft and down in the cellar. They even searched in the woods around the church, but no sign of him.

He was finally found when the service was over and everyone in the crowded church trooped out to the churchyard to bury the coffin. There was the sexton, fast asleep in the grave he'd dug that day. He'd had too much to drink and was snoring it all off, to the astonished eyes of all those people in black staring down at him.

Well, the good folk of the parish were pretty sore about that, for the man who had died was a well-respected man of the village. Some of the men got down there to heave the gravedigger up, which wasn't easy, as he was a solid sort of bloke and still limp with the drink. The story goes that, when they finally got him out, a great black raven flew over the churchyard. The sexton opened his blood-shot eyes in time to see the dark, flapping wings and sobered up pretty quick, running out of the churchyard hollering his head off. You see, ravens were thought to be a bad omen in those times. One flying anywhere over a church meant that there was certain to be a death soon. That sexton was so frightened he swore off the cider and started regular churchgoing, would you believe. As far as I know, he lived to a ripe old age, raven or no raven.

The raven wasn't a very popular bird, though. In the old mining days up on Dartmoor, it was a terrible thing to see one fly over the mine. If one flew over and its shadow passed over the shaft, it was a sure thing that someone would die. If ever they saw one of the birds, the men refused to go into the mine until everything was checked over to make sure it was safe.

There was once a miner who didn't believe in the old superstition. This man was the one who went boldly down into the shaft to check everything out when a raven flew over: he wasn't afraid of anything, especially not a bird. The others kept warning him that he was pushing his luck, but he took no notice, especially as he found nothing wrong underground despite the raven's flight over the mine.

This happened a few times, and after a while this man started to convince the other miners that ravens were just birds and not evil omens. Though still wary, they all started to be a bit careless when they saw a raven, not checking the mine, and so on.

As the story goes, what the miners didn't know was that the ravens were becoming furious at this arrogant miner. For centuries and centuries, the raven had been a symbol of warning, and here was this man taking no notice!

They gave him a chance. A warning. The king of ravens flew over the mine one day. It was the biggest bird anyone had seen, and even those who had been careless about these things refused to go down into the mine that day. Only that one man. He laughed at the others for being such cowards and went down there on his own. But this time, he found something wrong. A passage was wonky, and as he was coming back up, a load of dirt and rocks fell in the shaft behind him.

He'd had a lucky escape, but do you think he took the warning? Not a chance. The other miners did, and took heed every time they saw a raven, but not this fellow. He claimed it was nothing but a coincidence.

About a week later, not one but several ravens flew over the mine while the men were outside ready to go down. This was so unusual that all the men cowered in fear, refusing to budge. No one dared go down into the mine that day. No one, that is, except this one miner. Cocky as ever, he took no notice of the fearsome sign, of those ravens that were now perched on high rocks and tall trees around the mine, and walked brazen as you please into the mine.

The men stood outside all morning, waiting for the miner to come out. It was silent as the grave down in that underground shaft; not a sound came out of it. There wasn't a sound outside either. A wind that had come up in the morning, when the ravens were flying overhead, had stopped. Even the birds were quiet.

Then, all of a sudden, there was a loud whoosh as the ravens, quick as they'd come, all flew away, up in the sky and out of sight. That's what some of the miners said later anyway, but there were many who said different. They thought they saw the ravens fly into the mine itself, disappearing into the passageways. But it happened so fast, faster than the normal flight of birds, that they couldn't be quite sure.

An hour passed. No more ravens appeared, and things seemed more or less back to normal, so a few of the braver men ventured into the mine to see what had happened to their mate. What they found was terrible. The man was dead, deep down in the deepest mine shaft. He hadn't fallen, though, nor had there been any kind of mining accident. He looked as if he had been pecked to death by a dozen claws and beaks. By his body lay a single black feather. A raven's feather.

I can tell you this, my friends – those miners showed

respect for the ravens after that. They passed the story on to their sons who went down the mine, and they passed it down to the next generation, and so on, until the days of underground mining on the moor were finally over.

CHAPTER 8

Black Dog Inn

SO MANY STORIES THAT HAVE BEEN PASSED DOWN FOR centuries – some true, some tales and legends – are based around the local church or the pub, because they were the places everyone met, where much of the social life of the village took place. Sometimes too much socializing! My father used to tell of how the pub in West Buckland was shut because the farmer's tenants were spending too much time drinking in there. This was in about 1935.

The farmers themselves didn't mind a drink or two either. They used to come to the pub on their horses. Each time, they'd have too much to drink and by the time they left they were not sober by a long chalk, let me tell you. So the other farmers, the ones slightly more sober, would help out their drunken mate. They'd heave him on his horse then tie his feet together under the animal so he wouldn't fall off. Then they'd send him on his way, trusting that the horse knew its way home. Sometimes all the farmers had too much of the old demon cider and got their man on his horse back to front and sent him home without anyone noticing something was amiss.

Another feature of our villages in those days was the village policeman. The last one in High Bray was on the beat for seventeen years and made one arrest. This was one evening when he was on the bridge talking to his sergeant, passing the time discussing this and that. Suddenly, they caught sight of a poacher under the bridge, after the salmon. The sergeant sent the constable down there after that poacher. The policeman's face was stern and full of fury. He hissed at the poacher, 'Why didn't thee turn away, run for it? Now I got to arrest thee, as sergeant be on the bridge watching.'

It was a blot on his near perfect record, that one arrest, and he never forgave the poacher for it.

Along with the local policeman, each village had a tailor and a cobbler. I remember the cobbler in Brayford, sitting out in his shed, talking a blue streak while he worked. Even a mouthful of cobbles couldn't stop the flow; he could carry on a conversation with anyone who happened to call and not lose one of those cobbles from his mouth. It is well known that sometimes he'd pay the village children a few pence to keep tapping his hammer so that his wife would think he was still at work while he nipped off to the nearby pub. This happened often. I don't think his wife ever did find out. It was a great source of spare cash for the children of the village.

Our village had a carpenter too. He was a right laugh, a small man with a huge belly and white hair that stuck straight out from his head. He told visitors to the village that he made toilet seats to measure. He always told it with a straight face, asking if they'd like one made for them. The women always blushed red as beetroot as they stammered a refusal.

There was a blacksmith in most villages too. The smithy was a popular meeting place for the farmers and work-men. The children hung out there whenever they could, watching the sparks fly from the fire as the iron for the horseshoes was heated. I can still remember the ringing sound of the iron being hammered into shape. One of the blacksmiths was called Bill. Bill looked like the smithy he was, or what you'd imagine a smithy to be. He had a bushy black beard, and eyes as black as the coals on his fire. They had a spark in them too, for he was a fiery man. Bill, like the other blacksmiths, would mend anything as well as shoe a horse. He even pulled teeth for those who couldn't get to a dentist.

At the end of the day, if there was a horse that the farmer hadn't collected, he would just let it loose, give it a slap and send it home. The horse always found its way back to the right farm.

It was not only horses that found their way home, but other animals too. Dogs roamed about, stopping here and there for a bite to eat. One sheepdog liked a drop of cider now and again and used to visit the pub, where the landlord gave him a tiny bowl of the brew. The dog would drink up then make his way home to spend the rest of the evening snoring by the fire at his owner's feet.

In Dorset, there's a story of a great black hound dog that never left his owner's side. This was many years ago, way back in the seventeenth century, in a mansion near Lyme Regis. A very old and very lonely man lived in a great manor house there. His only friend was this black dog, who stayed with him day and night. But the dog wasn't able to save his owner the night that thieves broke into the manor. The hound somehow got locked in a downstairs room and couldn't get near the old man.

So the poor dog had to stand by helpless as the robbers dragged the man out of bed and began beating him senseless, trying to find out where he'd hidden his valuables. But the old man was so terrified he could hardly speak, even if he'd wanted to. This made the thieves so furious that they beat him until he was dead. Then, frightened at what they'd done, they rushed off, leaving the dog howling away and pining for his dead master.

Well, this is a very sad story, for the poor dog died of hunger in that house. It was several days before someone came to the manor and found the dead dog and the dead man.

The tale doesn't end there, no way. Over the years, that house was nearly destroyed. It was finally made into a farmhouse, round about the eighteenth century. Though much of it was ruined, the old fireplace in the parlour was still the same original one. And it was in front of the fire there one night that the new owner of the house, a farmer, got the surprise of his life. Sitting opposite him, curled up in a chair by the fireplace, was a great black hound dog!

The man was frightened to death, for he could tell it was no ordinary dog but a creature from another world. But after a time he began to lose his fear, for the dog just sat there and didn't seem to want to do any harm. The trouble was, the dog seemed to bring such a feeling of doom and gloom into the room. It was unsettling, to say the least.

This went on for several months. Some nights the dog would appear, in the same old chair by the fire, and some nights he wouldn't. But when he was there, he was always the same, never aggressive or bad-tempered. So you see, the farmer got used to him. But he was never really able to relax in that room. There was always a depressing feel around the place when that dog appeared, sort of gloomy and miserable. It was starting to spoil his evenings at home after his hard day's work out in the fields.

So this farmer started to go down to the local pub instead, where he told his neighbours all about his ghostly dog. They all advised him to get rid of the creature, saying it'd do him no good in the end, an animal from the spirit world lurking about his house. The farmer told them that the dog wasn't doing any harm, so why should he get rid of it? But the truth was, he was a bit afraid of what would happen if he tried to dislodge the animal. Still, he kept on defending the creature to his neighbours, and wouldn't listen to them for a long time.

But they kept on with him. They were getting a bit worried, you see, that this dog might harm the farmer. Finally, one night, the farmer had a bit too much to drink and decided he was fed up with being goaded about his dog. His anger turned on the dog for causing him so much trouble and worry. When he got home that night and saw that sodding dog curled up again in his usual chair, he lost his temper completely. He grabbed a poker and started chasing the animal. It ran up the stairs and finally into the attic, where the farmer had it cornered. But just as he was about to strike, the dog went right through the ceiling and disappeared.

The farmer, in a rage, and frightened too, seeing that dog vanish like it did, hit the ceiling with the poker. The blow made a hole in a part of the ceiling and – would you believe it? – down fell a wooden box. The farmer opened the box and inside were dozens of gold and silver coins. It was the most money he'd ever seen in his whole entire life!

Well, what luck! The farmer was now a very rich man. He bought a house on the Devon/Dorset border and turned it into an inn, which he called Black Dog Inn, in honour of the hound who'd found him the fortune. This is supposed to have been the first pub in Devon. It's closed now, but the house is still there. The dog doesn't haunt it, nor does he haunt that old farmhouse where his first master died. But he is still a restless spirit, so it seems. He took to haunting a little road near Black Dog Inn, which today is known as Dog Lane. People still say they know when that animal is around, because the lane feels cold and gloomy and eerie. You see, he's still sticking by his first master, not leaving the area where he lived happily with the old man.

CHAPTER 9

Black Hens and White Witches

MAY WAS FINALLY GETTING WARMER. IT'S A BUSY TIME FOR ME, with the safaris getting going on weekends. Sometimes I do two in one day, morning and afternoon. Then there's all the photographing I'd been doing. I'd been filming for a BBC4 programme, trying to get as many photos of birdlife as I could for it.

I'd been spending a lot of time on our land, watching all the wildlife come out in the springtime. It was a grand time of year to be there. There was so much going on. All the wildflowers were out and the woods and meadows were filled with primroses and, now, the bluebells. Wood anemones, too, and the white flowers of the wild garlic. I liked to spend hours in my hide, watching and photographing the deer that came around to drink water from our pond. The other animals too: badgers and hares; tiny fieldmice; weasels and stoats.

But it was the birds I was mainly trying to photograph this May, because of the television programme. Now, many people in our area knew of this project, and I had many well-wishers. It's amazing how many folk are interested in birdlife.

A farmer I met after a talk I gave in a village hall said to me, 'Now, Johnny, there's one bird I bet you'd never get a photo of in a million years.'

'Oh aye? So what bird's that then?' I asked.

He looked all mysterious like. 'The black hen of Dartmoor,' he said in a whisper.

I'd never heard of this black hen, but I knew there was a story there. 'All right, mate, so tell me about it.'

'Well, Johnny, many, many years back, there was a vicar in one of the villages who practised black magic. It was said he conjured up this black hen. Luckily, it's stayed the same size, for the story goes that, once, the gravedigger of the church got hold of the vicar's book of black magic and read out a spell that made that hen grow as high as a house. If it weren't for the vicar rushing home and changing the hen back, she'd still be roaming about Dartmoor like a big, black, feathered beast the size of a granite tor.'

I grinned. 'I've heard of all sorts of ghosts and things that haunt the West Country, but that's the first time I've heard of a chicken doing it.'

He laughed. 'I've heard tell of it for years; my father

told me first when I was a kid. The black hen always appears at twilight, in a small bit of meadowland on the south part of the moor. In the middle of this beautiful meadow there's a patch of lush green grass, and that's where people swear they've see the hen and her black chicks. If you get a photo of that, Johnny, it'll be something else.'

I shook my head. 'I'll wait hours and hours to get a photo of any real bird, but I'll be damned if I'm going to hang around waiting for the ghost of a sodding chicken, for goodness' sake!' He laughed, and so did I. As I left I said to him, 'Maybe one day someone will get a photo of that ghost hen, but it won't be me, that's for sure.'

Fortunately, most people are interested in real birds rather than ghost chickens and evil ravens. Julie's friend Helen is one of these. She was dotty about birds and wanted to help in my work with them. So she gave me this lovely Wendy box on my sixty-ninth birthday, back in February a couple of years ago. I couldn't believe it when I saw it. It was a very dainty little box, blue and grey and covered with flowers, the prettiest thing you ever saw. 'For birds,' Helen said. 'It's a Wendy box for birds.'

I thanked her, but I had to laugh, though. I said to Julie, 'It's a darn pretty box, but no birds will ever go in that one. It's so tiny!'

It was only about seven inches tall, with a sloping roof. It looked more like a toy than a proper bird box. But seeing that this young lady gave it to me, which was a thoughtful thing to do, I went on, 'Julie, I'll take this up to the land and fix it to the outside of our cabin.'

So I went and put it up, and forgot about it, thinking, That's it, nothing more will happen here. And it didn't for a whole year. But the following February – would you believe it? I still can't get my head around it, but eighteen wrens went into that box to roost. Eighteen! I had to bring Julie and all my family up to see this, and did I get a ribbing about it, for all the fun I made of it! As I said, it was a pretty little box, but I'd have bet my life that no bird would ever go in it. Shows how wrong a man can be.

Julie and I had bought a few cameras to go into the bird boxes, something I'd not done before, so I got many good photos after that.

There have been some rare fine days for birdwatching just lately, where the woods have been filled with birds of every sort, and the air with their singing and chattering. This time of year, they're all working away, making their nests, laying their eggs. There's a chaffinch made a nest in one of the hawthorn trees, and it's one of the prettiest little nests you've ever seen. It's made up of bits of moss, animal hair, wool and suchlike. Birds' nests are as varied as the houses people live in. The magpies' nests look like heaps of sticks all roughed up together any old how, with a roof on top.

It always gladdens me to hear birdsong, especially in springtime when all that business of nest-making is going on. The sparrows are chittering away, the thrushes and blackbirds singing louder than ever. Woodpeckers are tap-tap-tapping on the trees in my woods, and I've got swallows nesting in our tepee. When I'm there at night or in the very early morning, the air is filled with the hooting of the tawny owls. Ducks quack on the pond and the Canada geese have come back, with their honking, haunting cries.

The wild boars that come on to our land are good for the birds. They churn up the ground as they root for food and all the insects and bugs come out for the birds to feed on.

Not just the birds but the animals are busy as can be this time of year, mating, nesting, having babies. Rabbits everywhere, and foxes creeping around the trees. Badgers, too. Pheasants are everywhere, their distinct warning cry so sharp and clear when they sense danger.

I love photographing the animals, and I'm glad I don't hunt them instead, like I used to as a young man, especially when I hear about a hunter called Bowerman and the nasty thing that happened to him.

According to the legend, this Bowerman was a fantastic hunter. Any animal or bird he went for never stood a chance, for he never gave up until he got his prey. He was never without food, he and his family, for he was such a good hunter. When Bowerman and his hounds were out, people kept out of the way, because they knew nothing would stop them.

One day, the hunter and his hounds were bounding across Dartmoor, going after a hare, when they came upon a clearing full of witches. They were all in a circle, in the midst of some spell or another. The dogs should have left them alone, run around them or something, but instead they barged straight through the middle, spoiling their spell.

Oh, dearie me, the witches didn't like that, not one little bit! They had to have their revenge so, the next day, one of them mumbled some words of magic and turned into a hare. When this Bowerman and his hounds came out hunting, the hare ran right in front of them, attracting their attention straight away.

Of course, they all raced after this hare, thundering across the moor fast as can be. But a strange thing happened. For the first time ever, these hunters could not catch their prey. The hare had magical powers and just ran and ran until, finally, the hounds collapsed in a heap, completely exhausted. Bowerman kept on a little bit longer – he was a great, strong, tough man – but that hare was too much even for him. In the end, he was so worn out and tired that he fell to the ground, panting and trying to catch his breath, his muscles as weak as water.

The hare stood looking at him and, while he stared, amazed, it turned back into a witch. All the other witches came out from behind the rocks and hollows, and together they cast a spell on him and his hounds, turning them all into stones. Up on Dartmoor, you can still see the big rock they called Bowerman's Nose. And nearby is a cluster of smaller rocks known as Hound Tor.

*

Those witches weren't the first to turn one of their mates into a hare. There's another story about a hunter and a hare up on the moor. Only this story features several hunters and one very special hare.

This hare was known to everyone in the area as one of the biggest and fastest hares ever seen. It had great long ears and powerful back legs and could outrun hunters, horses and hounds without any trouble at all. Well, naturally, every hunter in the West Country wanted to be the one who got this hare. All the best ones would go up on the moor and have a go, but none of them could get near. It would outrun them all, no matter how many fresh hounds or fresh hunters came after it. Many a time they thought they had the creature cornered, but it would disappear, as if by magic, down some hole or some such.

Now, in this same area lived a witch. She had a little house on the edge of the moor and kept herself to herself. She was a nice witch, you see, and did no one any harm at all, so she was tolerated by all the villagers. They called her the white witch, for she never dabbled in black magic or played wicked tricks on people, like turning them into stone.

One day, a strange young man moved into the village. He was a fine hunter and seemed quite pleasant, so the locals accepted him. They told him about this rare and wonderful hare, bigger than any other, and how impossible it was to track him down.

Well, this man loved his hunting and prided himself on being a good hunter. He was determined to be the one to catch this fantastic creature. If anyone could, this man would be the one, everyone said, for his hunting ability was a legend all over England.

So he set off on his fine horse. It wasn't long before he spotted his prey. The villagers weren't exaggerating – it really was the most magnificent hare he'd ever seen, big and majestic-looking. The hunter gave chase. And, this time, the hare was wounded. That hunter managed to shoot an arrow into its back leg.

But, do you know, that hare kept right on going, with the arrow still stuck in its hind leg. Much to the hunter's surprise and frustration, the creature hardly broke its stride and, the next thing the man knew, the hare had disappeared into an underground passage between the granite rocks.

The next day, the hunter went out searching for the hare. He figured it couldn't live long, not with an arrow in its back leg. He was determined to bring his trophy home, but though he looked and looked, there was no sign of the hare.

Finally, tired and hungry, the hunter saw a little cottage on the edge of the moor. Thinking he might ask the owner for a bite to eat and something to drink, he knocked at the door. Imagine his surprise when the witch opened the door. The hunter wasn't frightened, though, as he remembered what folk around these parts had told him, that she was a friendly witch and never did harm to anyone.

The hunter asked for a place to rest for an hour or so,

and perhaps a bite to eat. The witch told him he could sit right there in the warm kitchen, in the chimney seat, and she would get him some food and drink. He thanked her gratefully and watched her as she turned and walked away from him. Her leg was bandaged up with a clean cloth but there was still a bit of blood seeping from the wound. And then he noticed something else. There beside the fire was an arrow. The hunter recognized it as his arrow, the one he'd let fly at the hare the day before.

He was so upset and confused, that man – you can imagine! He barely tasted the bit of bread and ale the witch gave him, and he could hardly look her in the face. He didn't linger there long, let me tell you. When he left the witch's house he went straight home and told no one about what had happened.

For a few weeks, the locals were saying that the hare must be dead, for there was no sign of it. But then one day it appeared, half hid behind a rocky outcrop. The hunters who were out that day had a go at chasing it, but by that time its leg had healed and it gave them the usual merry chase before disappearing.

No one ever got that hare. The only one who might have done, the new hunter who had moved to town, seemed to have gone off hunting, for he was never seen doing it again. Instead, he used to ride his horse for hours up on the moor, enjoying the scenery, I suppose. Every now and again one of the locals would spot him at the witch's cottage, sharing a spot of tea or suchlike together. Folk did talk then, wondering what a nice young man like that was doing hanging around with a witch. For, however friendly witches were, it didn't do to get too close to them.

The man didn't pay any attention to the talk, though, and never seemed to come to any harm by his acquaintance with the witch. He lived until a good old age and, when he died, the whole village came to his funeral. Nearly everyone there commented on the fact that the largest hare they'd ever seen had hopped out from behind the gravestones for a few seconds, and stood there, silent like, before turning and running back into the woodlands.

CHAPTER 10

Wee Willie Winkie and the Lady in Black

THE ODDEST THING HAPPENED LAST NIGHT DOWN AT THE PUB AT Bish Mill. A visitor from Porlock was telling a tale about a ghost that's said to haunt one of the old farmhouses outside North Molton. It's the ghost of an old man that folk have seen hanging out of the window of the house. 'I heard tell of that phantom ever since I was a boy,' said the man, who must have been about fifty years old. 'Even up at Porlock, people heard of that story.'

My ears were pricking up. I knew that farmhouse he was talking about. It was on a road I used to drive along in my young days, usually coming home from a night in the pub in a nearby village. I asked the bloke who was telling this story, 'So what's this ghost look like?'

He took a swallow of his cider. 'As I said, he's an old man. Must've lived centuries ago, because he's dressed in a long white nightgown and a white nightcap. You know, like Wee Willie Winkie in the kiddies' stories. The night-cap even has a bobble on the end. And he's got a long white beard.'

I ordered us each another drink. This story sounded damned familiar. 'So what's this ghost do?' I asked when we got settled again.

'Not much. There's this window above the door of the farmhouse and, on dark nights, sometime just after mid-night, people have seen him standing there, leaning out of the open window.'

'Bledy hell,' I said.

'What's up? Have you seen the ghost?'

I started to laugh. Several people turned to stare and smile at us, wondering what was going on. I didn't mind if they listened. This was a story too good not to be shared.

I told this man from Porlock that I knew exactly where the ghost story came from. Fifty odd years ago, when I was still a wild young man, I went out to the pub with a mate of mine named Ray. Now, we'd had a fair bit to drink, but in those days we didn't worry about drinking and driving. There weren't that many cars on the road, not out in our area, back then. And we didn't know any better, then. It didn't make it right, not by a long shot, but that's the way it was.

The road home was narrow and curvy, lots of nasty

bends. We hadn't gone far when a big black and white cow appeared right in front of us. It was a good job I wasn't going fast. I screeched on my brakes and the car came to a halt right behind her, missing her by about an inch.

Ray jumped out of the car and tried to get that cow to move out of the road, but she wouldn't dream of it. She trotted along right in front, Ray beside her, hollering for her to get out of the way, and me crawling along behind her in the car.

This went on for half a mile, and there were still a few miles of road left to get home. We had to get that sodding cow out of the road. There were some bad bends coming up, and anyone coming along fast in the opposite direction would get a right smash-up, hitting that creature. Not to mention us, following on behind her.

Ray and I were both relieved when the farmhouse came into view. We didn't know the folk who lived there, but we were hoping it was the owner of that cow. There weren't any other farms around, not for miles.

So there we were, at one in the morning, banging on this farmhouse door. It was all dark inside, everyone asleep. Suddenly, the window right above my head opened up wide and this man poked his head out. He had a white beard, and a white bobble nightcap on and looked like Wee Willie Winkie, as I said to Ray later. We had a hard time keeping from laughing as we explained about the cow; he looked so damn funny in that long white nightshirt.

There was silence for a few moments at our table when I finished that tale. Then the man from Porlock said, 'Johnny, you saw that ghost!'

'He was no more a ghost than I am,' I said. 'Don't you see what's happened? Ray and I told everyone later about the man who looked like the ghost of Wee Willie Winkie. I guess folk told others, and that's how the story of a haunting at that farmhouse began.'

The man from Porlock looked doubtful. 'Well, Johnny, what if it's the other way around? What if you *thought* you were talking to a living farmer, but it was really the ghost?'

I shook my head. 'I don't think so, mate.'

But I can tell he didn't believe me. And I'll bet you anything, soon word will get around that Johnny Kingdom saw that phantom of the farmhouse, on a dark and mysterious night over fifty years ago.

But thinking on it, what if I did? That would be a laugh on me, wouldn't it, if it really was the ghost?

Thinking of these things later, I wonder if that's how many of the ghost stories get started. Maybe in a hundred years from now, the ghost of Wee Willie Winkie will be said to haunt that old farmhouse where we saw that white-bearded man. Or, even better, in that pub where the story was told.

Heaven knows, there are hundreds of stories of haunted pubs in the West Country. In North Devon, there's a pub called the Coach and Horses that dates back to the thirteenth century which was once used as a courtroom. There was a damp, nasty jail in the cellar and the room behind the bar was said to be an execution chamber. Not what a decent pub should have, by a long shot! So, of course, there is at least one ghost there lurking around.

The one most seen is a lady in black. She wanders around the room that used to be the courtroom, and also up and down the corridors. I heard tell of two people, a Cornish man and his wife who were up in Devon for a visit, who swear they saw her.

This man and his wife were staying for a few days near this particular pub. One night, they spent the whole evening there, relaxing after a long day sightseeing. At first, it was all nice and jolly. The pub was full, and everyone was feeling in a holiday mood. The trouble was, when it got late and many of the customers said goodnight and left for home, this Cornishman didn't want to know. He was on holiday and having a high old time, and wanted to carry on partying.

His wife was getting pretty sore by now. She was tired and wanted her bed, but she felt she should try to prise her man from the local brew, which was pretty potent. She knew her sightseeing the next day would be out of the question, him having the hangover of his life.

So it wasn't much fun for her by then. Finally, she gave up trying to get her husband home and left him to it. She decided to go back to the B&B where they were staying, and said she'd see him there. The man said he'd be back soon, but when he didn't turn up, the wife, getting completely fed up by now, went back to the pub to drag him out.

It was nearly closing time and the pub almost empty. The wife said later that there was a strange atmosphere in the place. She couldn't describe it exactly, but the air seemed sort of misty, unreal, she said. It made her feel uneasy, though she didn't know why.

At first she couldn't see her husband. Then, looking around, she saw him right at the end of the bar, with a strange woman perched beside him. The woman was dressed all in black, her face hidden by a kind of dark scarf or shawl. Her hair, too, was black and also helped hide her face.

This woman was sitting far too close to the husband. Why, any nearer and she'd be in his lap! The wife watched while the stranger leaned in even closer, letting her hair brush against the husband's cheek. 'She seemed to have taken a fancy to him,' the wife told everyone back home later. 'Not that he was anything to look at. A stone overweight, for a start. But there she was, falling all over him like he was God's gift.'

The wife, a feisty Cornishwoman, was absolutely furious. Who was this woman falling all over her husband? She stepped forward, all set to go over and give the lady in black a piece of her mind. But before she could get to him, the lights suddenly went out and the room was in total darkness. The wife gave a little shriek, it had happened so sudden like. She could hear the bartender muttering, 'What's happened to the lights?' and her husband saying, 'Must be a power cut.'

The odd thing was that there was a moon that night, and a light outside the pub door, but somehow no light managed to get through the windows. The darkness was black as tar. But before anyone could do anything, the lights suddenly came on again. The wife saw the bartender, and her husband, but no one else in the pub. The strange woman had gone.

'Where is she then?' the wife cried. 'Where's your floozy gone?'

The husband looked at her as if she'd lost her mind. 'What're you on about?' he wanted to know.

'I saw her, falling all over you. How did she get out? No one got out past me, I would've heard her. Those high-heel shoes she was wearing would've clattered like hell on this floor.'

The husband and bartender stared at the woman, and at each other. The bartender said, 'There was no one here, ma'am, only your husband. I was having one last drink with him before closing up.'

The wife told them both what she'd seen. They swore there hadn't been a woman in that pub since she left. There were a few other blokes for a short time but then they left too. She called her husband a rotten liar. When the bartender tried to stick up for him, she told him to keep quiet. The husband finally said she was crazy. They had a standing-up row, which was talked about in the village for weeks.

The funny thing about this story is that a couple of the blokes who had been in the pub came back for some cigarettes just before the wife came in. When they heard the story the next day, they too swore blind that what the husband said was true. No one had seen the woman but the wife.

Luckily, those same blokes were smoking outside the pub when the angry couple, still arguing, came out. They couldn't help but overhear, and what they heard made the cigarettes drop right out of their mouths! The woman had seen the pub ghost, no doubt about it.

They stopped the couple, and tried to explain to the wife that she must have seen the spirit of the Lady in Black who haunted the Coach and Horses. And do you know, she wouldn't believe them. She told her friends at home, 'Not only did he lie, he got the whole pub to lie with him! Men are all the same, sticking together at times like those.'

It was only after a few weeks that she finally accepted she'd actually seen a ghost. When they got home, her husband told her how he had felt something touch his face several minutes before the lights went out. He even tried to brush it away, thinking it was a tiny spider's web or some such thing, but there was nothing there. It kept irritating him, whatever was brushing against him, and he kept trying to wipe it away, until the lights went out and the strange sensation stopped. He was so unnerved about the whole thing that he didn't want to go near a pub for the next month or so, which is when his wife began to believe his story.

That ghost, that troublesome Lady in Black – she was very mischievous, getting that man into all sorts of trouble with his wife.

But at least not all pub ghosts are mean spirits. In Shebbear, there's a pub called The Devil's Stone which is haunted by a young girl and a friendly old man with a grey beard. The place has been an inn since around 1600, and they say there's a tunnel running from the pub to the church, which is nearby. Or there used to be, anyway. I heard tell that the clergy from the church used the tunnel to pop into the inn for a quick nip without their congregation seeing them go into the drinking establishment.

Another story I heard was that a monk from somewhere abroad – France, I think it was – got so hooked on the Devonshire brew that one morning he had so much to drink he forgot where he was and began a service in the pub! The drinkers were so chuffed that this man of God had come to their pub in order to save their souls – or so they thought! – that they praised him to the high heavens. And instead of being thrown out of the Church, this clergyman went back to France a hero.

So the story goes, anyhow. I don't know how much of it is true, but then that's the same with so many stories, the ones that go back centuries anyway. They grow like great oak trees from a tiny acorn of truth.

But this one must be true. The man who told me got it from his father, who got it from his grandfather, who grew up in Shebbear. You can't get closer than that to a tale.

CHAPTER 11

Cart Horses and a Murder Mystery

UP ON EXMOOR THE OTHER DAY, I PASSED NEAR TO CODSEND Moor. This part of Exmoor is mostly rough ground, full of bogs and mud and mire, not the best kind of place for hikers and visitors even now.

Something terrible happened up around here long ago, and even now sometimes folk talk about it, wondering exactly what happened. This was back in the 1920s, when this part of the moor, covering about 150 acres or so, must have been even more bleak and desolate than it is now. To this day, it's still a mystery why a seventeen-year-old girl called Mollie Phillips went there and why and how she died there. She'd set out from the farm she was working at near Exford, having the afternoon and evening off, saying she was off to visit her aunt in Cutcombe. She never got there, and she didn't go back to the farm either. Before she left, she'd promised the housekeeper she'd be home before dark, but the woman was the last anyone saw of that poor maid.

It was in September, and the weather was nice and sunny. The girl was healthy and fit, according to the old stories. She didn't have a boyfriend, didn't seem to have an interest in boys, nor in anything much except her work on the farm and her family. It was a proper mystery, for she knew the way to her aunt's house and there was no reason to suspect she'd got lost.

When she didn't get home by dark, the housekeeper was cross but didn't worry. She thought the girl had decided to skive off from work and spend the night with her aunt. It wasn't like her, but who knew, maybe she'd taken ill or something. But when the girl didn't show up the next day, the housekeeper sent word to the aunt's house asking where she was.

Of course, she'd never arrived. The aunt hadn't worried either, for she assumed her niece had decided not to come over that day. But now everyone realized that the girl was missing.

A huge search party set off from the Crown pub in Exford. I've seen an old 1929 photo of it. There're over twenty men and women, most on horseback, setting out to search for the missing girl. It's a proper old-fashioned-looking group, with the women side-saddled on the horses, the men wearing suits and ties and proper hats.

But, in their hearts, I'm sure there was the same fearsome worry that anyone would have today, if a youngster disappeared like Mollie did.

The search party didn't find a thing. Not a trace of her. Bigger search parties were organized all that autumn until a 50-mile area around Exford had been covered. And still nothing. The locals kept saying, 'It's as if she's vanished into thin air,' and some were even saying she'd been whisked away by the Exmoor mists and fogs that filled the hills and valleys that autumn, tempted there no doubt by the troublesome pixies that inhabited those parts.

It wasn't until fifteen months later that a farmer and his workman found her remains in a small spring on the moor, on one of the boggy bits. They'd been up on the moor, burning off some long grass, and found a human skull and some bones. Some of her clothing too.

To this day, no one has solved the mystery of Mollie Phillips. There was an inquest and an inquiry, and even the national newspapers were full of speculation. Many folk thought she'd been murdered, or else had run in panic from someone and tripped and fell, hitting her head. Doctors and pathologists were consulted, but everyone differed.

There was certainly something odd about what happened. For a start, where she ended up was not on the way to her aunt's place. There was no way she'd have gone across Codsend Moor to get there. So either she had no intention of seeing her aunt, and lied to the housekeeper, or else she'd been dragged, or enticed, or scared, into the spot where she was killed.

No one believed for a minute that Mollie had been going to meet someone and had told a fib to the house-keeper. There was no boyfriend on the scene at all, nor anyone else she could possibly have met – not that anyone knew about anyway.

There was another strange thing – the way a stone was placed on the body, some people thought it must have been put there. The way they found the bones, too, looked like she might have fallen on her face while running away, and then the bog had sucked her down.

But what was she running away from, if that was the case? And why so far from where she was supposed to be? And was that bog deep enough and dangerous enough to kill a person, or was she held down until she died?

The arguments about whether the bog at Codsend could suck a person to their death went on and on for months. Some locals said no way – it was no more than a puddle of water, a small spring, and in all the years they lived there, no one or nothing had gone there and not been able to get out. Others said the opposite, that they knew of horses and cows that had been sucked into the peaty bog. All these locals had their say at the inquest. Everyone had an opinion and tempers grew fiery as people tried to force their verdicts on others.

The story never did die. The inquest's verdict was death by misadventure, but it was thought someone or something had frightened her into the bog. She'd died of exposure and possibly drowning, that was the official statement.

This wasn't the end, though. A powerful and well-known local vicar got into his pulpit the day of Mollie's funeral and said it was murder down and out, that Mollie's body had been dumped in that bog. He said that a strong and healthy girl who knew the moor well, had roamed it since childhood, was not about to wander carelessly into a bog that probably didn't exist anyway, as the September of the year she died had been exceptionally dry.

That vicar, he got a lot of support. Reporters from all the London newspapers came to interview him, and he got hundreds of letters of encouragement. The mystery of Mollie Phillips was even brought up in the House of Commons. And it all stemmed from the question that even now folk disagree about – can a bog on Exmoor be so treacherous as to suck a strong creature down to his or her or its death – or not?

The vicar even offered £20 to the local hospital, a grand old sum in those days, if someone would offer to throw him in the bog and he didn't get out within five minutes. As far as I know, no one took him up on it. As for me, I don't know. I've never seen an animal get sucked down to its death on the moor, though I've been in bogs when my foot has gone right down through the peat and turf. I might've had a hell of a muddy boot and foot, but I've never been in danger of getting stuck.

Still, you never know. Exmoor is full of secrets and mystery and I always like to keep an open mind about the stories I hear.

The other day, I was talking to an old boy who knew my father from when he was a lad. He'd come over to me at my stall in the market at South Molton on a Thursday morning to pass the time away.

There're many wonderful people who stop and have a chat at the market every week. It's in the old indoor marketplace, a good place to be if the weather is wet, as it often can be. There are a good many stalls, people selling everything from plants to home-made cakes, tools, small items for the house, all sorts of odds and sods. Julie and I take my DVDs and books and photos to sell, and we meet all sorts of interesting folk. Sometimes they're locals, friends and suchlike, and others are strangers. It's always good to talk to all of them.

This man I was talking about, Davey is his name. He doesn't come often now because he's got too much bothering him, bad hips and knees and suchlike. The cold gets to him, so it's got to be a good day when he comes out.

Spring had finally started to warm up so Davey's aches and pains had eased a bit and he came into market one fine day. As he always does, he started in talking about the good old days. Now, I love that kind of talk, as anyone who knows me will testify. But the market was crowded with people that day, both visitors and locals. Because I got a bit known doing my series on wildlife for the BBC, there were folk standing around buying my books and DVDs and others out on a daytrip and wanting no more than a chat, which was fine by me.

And there was this tiny old man – he's short and bent and skinny – not wanting to move from in front of my stall. Luckily, Julie was with me, as she always is, so she was able to talk to the visitors and do the business while I had my usual conversation with Davey.

'Remember that farm we used to work on, Johnny? Outside the village?'

He was speaking of the time when I was sixteen and working on my first farm. Davey, a young man then, was doing odd jobs for the farmer too. We started talking about those old days when all the work was done by cart horses. They're wonderful creatures, sturdy and sound. When I first started on that farm, we worked with a horse and butt – a small cart – but later the farmer got an old Fordson Major tractor.

Davey didn't like it much when tractors came in. He loved those cart horses. He had a few acres of his own, kept a few animals for himself and to sell to the villagers for meat. A few sheep, a pig. A couple of calves. It's hard to do that nowadays with all the rules and regulations, all the forms to fill out. But then, anyone with an acre or two, or even a big garden, kept something to help with the feeding. Even if it was no more than a few hens for the eggs.

This Davey had saved up his money and got a horse

and butt for himself. Later, he lived higher up on Exmoor and got himself a bit more land. 'I never did get no tractor for my land,' he said to me. 'I loved those old workhorses. Mind, I had one that was always playing tricks on me.'

'What sort of tricks?' I asked.

'Oh, the usual. Like mules, them cart horses can be. Stubborn as hell. Stopping if they feel like it, for no reason at all. This one I had used to neigh as if he was starving when I knew he'd packed away more'n enough grub. Good, solid, sturdy thing, let me tell you. He'd trick me into getting out more feed and do no more than nibble at it.'

Davey was gazing out over the marketplace, not seeing the stalls, the stallholders, the crowds of people. He was in another world with his old cart horse. He went on, 'That horse played a right bloody trick on me at the end, though. He was hitched up to the butt and we were going up this steep hill on the moor. All of a sudden, the horse started panting and, before I could do a thing, he dropped on to his knees. Minutes later, down he plopped all the way. "Damn," I said. "He's dead."'

Davey shook his head, still bewildered, after all these years, by the death of that horse. 'Johnny, I was that shocked. He'd never played that trick on me before.'

I peered into the old man's face to see if he was pulling my leg, but he looked serious and sort of sad too, still thinking about his poor dead horse. I said, 'No, Davey, I suppose he never did. It'd be hard as hell to play that same trick twice, even for a cart horse as smart as yours.'

CHAPTER 12

The Devil and His Cider

FRANKLYN'S DAYS ARE 18, 19 AND 20 MAY, AND IT WAS NEARLY that time now. There's a good story behind Franklyn's Days, one I've known from childhood.

It seems that a brewer bought a large quantity of barley from a local farmer. Now, the devil was well aware that Devon was noted for its cider, and he wasn't very happy about that. He was afraid it would spoil the sale of beer and, of course, beer was important to the devil. We all know what mischief occurs, what devilment, when too much beer and cider is consumed on a Saturday night.

So the devil went to this brewer who'd bought the barley. 'Now, look,' he said, 'we've got to be careful here. There's too much good cider being made in Devon, and your beer sales are going to go right down.'

The farmer nodded, scratched his head. 'You're telling me, mister? It's a fair old worry, let me tell you. Keeps me awake at night, but what do I do? I'm a brewer.'

'I'll tell 'ee what to do,' said the devil. 'All you have to do is sell your life and soul to me. I'll cause a nasty blight to ruin the apple crop. How's that for a deal?'

'Sounds like a good deal,' the brewer said after some thought. 'My life and soul won't be worth a penny if my beer won't sell. My wife'll leave me, my kids will hate me, and my debtors will string me up on the nearest apple tree.'

'So it's a deal?' the devil asked, smacking his red-hot lips.

'It's a deal.'

They shook hands on it. The brewer had to run and put his fingers under cold water, they were that scorched, but the deal was done.

And so it was arranged that, from then onwards until the end of time, there would be three days and nights of cold wind or frost just around the time when the apple trees were in blossom. Sure enough, it happens year after year, and this is why we've always been told not to put out any plants till after Franklyn's Days.

That story must be fairly common around the combes and hills of Exmoor, because Julie had heard it too when she was growing up. I wondered if the brewer's name had been Franklyn, but his name was never mentioned. Probably it was. That Franklyn, if it was the brewer, he made a rotten deal. No matter how much cider is made, there are always those that love their beer. As one who has enjoyed both in my lifetime, I know what I'm saying.

There was once a monk who nearly sold his soul for some sweet cider. This happened at an old abbey in Devon, in a place called Tavistock. In long-ago times, the monks at the abbey made cider, and good stuff it was too. But, by and by, some of them thought that their cider was a bit sharpish and set about trying to make a sweeter version. Now, one of the monks was called Brother John and, of all the monks, he loved cider the best – especially sweet cider. So he was determined to make some.

In those days, the only way to make a sweet cider was to add a bit of wine to it. The trouble was, wine was expensive to make and the abbey needed to keep its supply for important occasions, like when the bishop or some such person came to visit. It couldn't be used just for making cider for the monks, so you can see there was a bit of a dilemma.

Brother John decided that he was the one to solve the problem. He would be the one to find out how to make a sweet cider without using up the wine. He didn't quite know how he'd do this, but he made up his mind that he would try. And so he made many batches of the stuff, trying this and that, but none of it turned out sweet.

Then he got lucky. A new worker appeared at the abbey. He was a tiny little man, very strange-looking, but he was eager to work. He told the abbot he would do any-thing as long as he had a bit of food and a place to sleep for the night. The abbot offered him a bed, but the stranger said all he needed was an empty wine cask. It was round and warm and cosy and he could fit in comfortably.

Well, would you believe, this little man was actually the devil in disguise. He was put to work helping Brother John with the cider, and every day he whispered temptations in the monk's ear, saying that if he could have John's soul, he'd teach him the secret of making sweet cider without wine.

It was that hard for Brother John to resist, for sure. How he loved his sweet cider! Then, one day, he nearly caved in. The funny old man went on and on at him, talking about the brew he could help John make, how wonderful it would be. But just as John was about to give in to temptation, he caught a whiff of sulphur coming from the old fellow's hair. He realized that this was the devil that was tempting him, and told him in no uncertain terms to get back to hell, where he belonged.

The devil was furious, but instead of going back to hell he crawled back inside the wine cask where he slept at night. He figured he'd nearly got Brother John's soul that day, and it was only a matter of time before the monk would give in.

But the devil hadn't reckoned on what a fighter that John was! Determined to get rid of the nasty bloke once and for all, Brother John sealed up the cask and started pouring cider in it, hoping to drown the devil. What a fury that imp kicked up! He swore and kicked the barrel and thrashed about like, well, like the devil himself. He got that cider churned up like crazy before he'd had enough and disappeared back to hell.

When all the fuss inside the barrel had died down, Brother John opened the cask. The first thing he noticed was the smell. It smelled like hell itself, all sulphur and fire and brimstone. He nearly tipped the whole lot out then and there but, like I said, Brother John loved cider and couldn't resist having a jug of it before tipping it away.

To his surprise, it was a sweet cider, and tasted wonderful. He'd found a way of making the stuff without wine – you just poured it over sulphur, or so the story goes. From then on, the cider was known as 'matched' cider, which meant it was made from the same stuff matches were.

Brother John had a high old time of it that night, drinking a good portion of the sweet cider in that barrel. But he saved some for the abbot to taste, who praised him highly for his discovery. The monk never told anyone about the devil's part of it, but word must have leaked out somewhere. I'm telling it now, aren't I!

CHAPTER 13

Haunted Places Both Indoors and Out

THAT EVENING, JULIE AND I DROVE OUT TO BRAY TOWN AGAIN. Seeing Davey at South Molton market, and talking to some of the other old-timers there had got to me. Maybe we all need to go back to our childhood roots when we get older, like touching base with something deep inside us.

I've never gone far, mind. The distance between High Bray and Bishops Nympton is only a dozen miles, give or take a few either way. Julie and I still live in the council house we moved into a few months after we married. We own it now. It's always been home to us and I hope it always will. It's round about fifty years ago when we first moved in. Hard to believe.

There was no particular reason why we were heading back to the place where I was born. After the South Molton market we had gone home, had some dinner and then I'd gone out to Anstey Common again to try to get a photo of that darned cuckoo. I could hear him out there – cuckoo, cuckoo – almost like he was mocking me. Cuckoo, come find me if you can.

No luck again that time, though I did get some photos of a stag and a hind standing on the high moor, a late-afternoon mist swirling up behind them like ghosts coming out of the wooded cleave.

While I think of it, there's a real ghost of a stag that haunts a part of Devon, or so someone once told me. It haunts the dual carriageway that bypasses the town of Okehampton. This road was built across an ancient deer park, and there was a big protest about it at the time. In the end, despite the protests, the road cut through these old woodlands anyway, right on the edge of the moor. Now and again, though, a motorist has seen a huge white stag standing on the side of that road. It looks real, and so magnificent, really huge and in the prime of life. But the driver of the vehicle, and any passenger, gets the shock of their lives when they pass by and find out that they can see right through this stag! Its form is still there, but it's a ghostly, white, misty shape of a deer.

Some farmers say they have seen it in their fields too. They see this beautiful deer standing proudly in the middle of a grassy meadow, and they stand and stare at it, then suddenly it disappears. I don't mean it turns tail and runs, like deer do, but it vanishes into the air, *poof!*, just like that.

One farmer's wife took a photo of the white stag, or tried to. She thought she got a great shot on her digital camera but, when she looked, there was nothing there. Her grown daughter saw the stag at the same time, though, so she knew she wasn't seeing things.

Anyway, the mist followed us steadily in clumps as we drove around some of the villages near Brayford, places I'd played in, fought in, chased the girls in, drank in (they all had their local pubs) and worked in too. Digging graves with my father, working on farms and timber yards. Poaching, too, and catching moles to sell for their skins. Any old thing, to make a bit of cash, which was sorely needed in those days, as I've said many times.

Driving around all the places I hung out in as I was growing up, I noticed how all the old ramshackle houses had been done up: new thatch, posh lanterns outside the doors, that sort of thing. Years ago, no one had the money to do up their houses. I remember big old fireplaces looking as if they'd not changed for a couple of hundred years, with water dripping down from a leaking chimney. Some houses still had a hole in the wall by the fire where you put hot ashes. The women who lived in these places still put cloam bowls filled with milk in those holes and, before long, it would turn into rich, delicious cream. It was so tasty, that cream, eaten with home-made scones and jam, that it didn't matter that there were buckets all over the place to catch the drips in the ceiling, or that the wooden window frames were so rotten that if you put your finger on them they'd crumble to the touch.

I remember several houses like that from my child-hood; in fact, we were passing one now. I opened the window to see it more clearly. It's been done up as a second home for someone now, looking all smart and polished. The family who'd owned it all those years ago wouldn't have recognized it. It's not that the folk who lived there were lazy or anything, there was just no extra cash for much else beside food. But the food that there was was so wholesome and delicious. Faggots of wood were put into that wall oven and, when it got piping hot, out would come the ashes from the fire and in would go the bread or cakes, the pasties or fruit pies. Lovely grub! I used to visit the family just in time for tea, when the missus made her cakes and stuff. We kids polished it off quick as you could whistle. 'That woman in that house over there made the best food I've ever eaten,' I said out loud, thinking about it.

Julie looked at me sideways and I added quick as a flash, "Course, I mean second-best grub. Or third. Yours has got to be right up there on top, Julie. Along with me mum's, naturally.'

That was close. You don't get to be my age, and married to one woman as long as I have, without learning how to say the things they want to hear sometimes.

The story of that family I used to visit did not end happily. The father had some kind of accident with the farm machinery and died when the children were still young. The family soon moved away and the house was empty for a long time. I think one of the reasons no one bought it right away was because of the ghost.

A neighbour saw it first. He was walking by the place late at night and saw a light inside, in the big room where the fireplace was. Thinking it was youngsters fooling around, he went to make sure they weren't doing any damage. He looked into the window and nearly had a heart attack. There, standing by the cold, empty fireplace, was Mr Todd, looking as alive as he was.

The neighbour ran like hell out of there, but was back shortly with several other men. He'd convinced himself that it was only someone who looked like Mr Todd, and that it was only some tramp bedding down for the night. But he wanted to make sure.

Four other men saw the ghost of Mr Todd that night. They all looked through that same window, and they all said the same thing. It was no other than Mr Todd. The thing was, they'd all gone to his funeral, had seen him dead and buried.

They were frozen in terror, those four big, grown men. And as they watched, the ghost slowly disappeared right in front of their eyes.

The next day, the house was as it was before: dark and empty and going to ruin. No one ever saw the ghost again, but now and then a light would appear in one of the rooms. It would go on mysteriously in the middle of the night, and sometimes still be on the next day before vanishing before noon. Sometimes noises could be heard too, the noise of a man crying.

No one went near that house for a long time.

There's another haunted house I've heard of in Somerset, in a small village. There's a very old thatched house there, opposite a church. Ages ago, this was the house where the priest of the church lived.

This man was no doubt a very good priest, but then something happened. He fell in love, you see, and priests weren't allowed to do that. To make it worse, the woman he loved was a nun. She loved him back, and ran away from her convent to be with him. They decided to break their vows and marry. They had to do this in secret, though, so he made a hidden room for her in this big old house, which she never left. It was their hiding place from the world.

One day, though, the priest was called away somewhere, on some kind of church business, and when he got back, his wife was dead. He never knew how or why she died. Of course, she had to be buried and the priest had to tell his secret. You can imagine the ruckus it caused! It was never discovered what killed her and the mystery remains to this day. The house is still there and there is a ghost that haunts it. It's the figure of a monk who has been seen wandering about the place. There is also a strange knocking that goes on which seems to come from nowhere; people who live in the house have heard it often. No one knows if the ghostly monk and the knocking are the priest looking for his lost wife, but it sure as hell sounds like it. Can't think of what else it could be.

Sometimes it seems like all of the West Country is full of haunted houses. I think maybe it's because, long ago, this part of the world was so isolated from the more populated eastern side of the country. It took days and days for news from London to arrive, and for people from there to arrive too. And, of course, there were the moors, Dartmoor and Bodmin as well as Exmoor, which in those days were wild and rough, cut off from the rest of the world. So these isolated houses dotted around the West Country were ripe for tales of mystery and haunting.

In Devon, there's a big house called Lewtrenchard Manor, which has quite a few ghosts lurking around. The place was built in the early seventeenth century, but the best-known ghost story comes from the 1700s. A young woman called Susannah was married there at the manor one March day. Unfortunately, that poor young girl dropped dead of a heart attack right after her wedding ceremony. She was walking along the long drive up to the house and down she fell, just like that, dying on the spot. Since then, Susannah has been seen often, walking up and down that drive in her wedding dress. She is a very sad and unhappy ghost, as you can imagine.

About forty or fifty years after that, a woman called Margaret took over the property after her son had lost most of the family fortune by gambling it all away. The only thing that was saved was the manor house, though it was left in a near-derelict state.

This Margaret was a smart woman. She had a business sense that would be envied by many people today. She worked hard and paid back all her son's gambling debts. Not only that, but she also made many improvements, slowly doing up the house so that it was the way it had been before. She loved her home, you see, and, when she died, she couldn't leave it. Her ghost is said to still be there, wandering up and down the big gallery of the house.

As if two ghosts weren't enough, Lewtrenchard Manor is said to have a third. Later on, a squire owned it and lived there for many years, keeping it in top-notch condition, repaired and cleaned and as perfect as he could get it. This squire married a young girl from the mills who he had met when she was only sixteen. He had her educated first, mind, before he married her, so as not to take advantage of her, most likely. Then he finally married her, and they lived happily for forty-eight years. Would you believe, they had fifteen children!

This squire is the manor's third ghost. He's another one of the residents that so loved the house that he can't seem to leave. He's often seen wandering about outside in the grounds, keeping an eye on the place and making sure that the present owners keep it in good repair.

There's another big country house in Cornwall, too, that is haunted by several ghosts. This is Lanhydrock House in Bodmin. It was built nearly four hundred years ago but most of it was ruined by a terrible fire around a hundred and fifty years ago. The lord and lady who owned the house passed on soon after. In fact, the woman died right after the fire. She'd been rescued from an upstairs window, but the shock killed her. About a year later, her husband passed on, probably from a broken heart.

Now, this couple had one son, Thomas, who rebuilt the house and even the church that had been destroyed by the fire, for his parents had loved that church too. He did a fine old job, for the house is restored today and open to the public. Many ghosts have been seen there, but no one seems sure who they are. The most frequently seen ghost is that of a little old lady. She's dressed in grey and has been spotted sitting in some of the rooms. The spooky thing is that she doesn't look like a ghost. She looks like a real live woman who is dressed in the costume of that time. But when people go up to her, and get close, she suddenly vanishes! That's when they know they've seen a ghost. It must put the fear of God into whoever sees this vanishing spirit. I suppose it could be the ghost of the lady who died after the fire, but I don't think she was that old. Maybe she aged years and years in the few days she lived after that terrible event.

There are many other strange hauntings in this house. Some people have heard a girl giggling in the nursery, and others have seen the ghostly figure of a man wandering around in the gardens. Other ghosts have been seen in nearly every room. If ever there was a haunted house, Lanhydrock surely is one of them.

CHAPTER 14

Witches and Suchlike

I'VE BEEN UP EARLY THESE LAST FEW MORNINGS, OUT AND ABOUT taking photos of some hinds getting ready to calve. Late May, and the dawn light creeping through that ghostly mist, still hanging around in mornings and evenings, is something to see. The yellow gorse flowers looked on fire in the sunrise.

I found the hinds I was looking for, and it was fantastic – one of them had her little baby and I got some good shots of the newborn, a little brown fawn with white spots, pretty as a picture, just like Bambi. No one but me out at that time, the only sounds that of skylarks chirping away and a buzzard making his peculiar call as he circled overhead.

It was a lucky day for me. After I'd finished with the

deer I was ambling back to my jeep, eyes popping out all over my head as they do when I'm on the lookout for wildlife, when all of a sudden two long ears poked out from behind a stumpy hawthorn bush. It was a hare. Now I've filmed hares before. I've been lucky enough to film two of them boxing. But hares are not like rabbits: you don't see them all over the place. So I was pleased to see this one. I stood there frozen while it jumped out from behind the bush. To my surprise, it jumped towards me, not away. I had my camera ready. I hoped I caught that look of surprise on that hare's face as he spotted me. With another jump, he tore off in the opposite direction. It was wonderful watching it leap. Rabbits run, hares leap. They've got these great thumping back legs; powerful.

I was near Exford then so I stopped in the town. If there's a capital on Exmoor, it's got to be Exford, right in the middle of the moor. It's a small town, much smaller than Dulverton or Dunster. Several pubs, village shop and post office, couple of cafés open in summer. Great little place, the river going through it, the moor all around.

I'd eaten my sandwiches up on the moor, drunk the tea in my flask, but it was getting towards midday and I was thirsty. The day had turned warm, the mist gone. On my way into the pub I met a man I knew from the old days. He'd worked on farms like I had, but I'd not seen him for years. Fernley is his name.

So we settled down for some talk and a pint. We got to chatting about days gone by. He said, 'Remember Iris? That old lady living in the shed in the middle of nowhere?

Can't remember exactly where. Somewhere a few miles out of South Molton, anyway.'

I vaguely remembered. Fernley went on, 'I did odd jobs for her now and again, when my folks moved to South Molton. I used to cycle up to her place. Weren't nothing there, just a sodding shed with a tin roof.'

'She lived there for years, didn't she?' I asked.

'For donkey's years. Tough as old boots, she was. Must've been ninety when I went there.'

I was starting to remember. 'She was still driving then. All us lads used to jump out'a her way when she came in to market in South Molton. Had a beat-up pick-up truck, old as the hills. Used to come in to collect her groceries, and get a new Calor gas cylinder for her fire.'

I took a swig of cider. Nothing more refreshing after a warm morning's work. Fernley said, 'I was always terrified I'd find her froze there in winter. I'd cycle up, scared shitless I'd find a corpse in that bed in the shed, but she'd be up and about, poking around outside with her old tabby cat.'

I remembered that cat. I'd gone up there once, probably with Fernley, and that cat was fearsome. Old as Iris, and tough as nails. Hissed like crazy when anyone came round. Better than a goose or a guard dog any day – or would've been, if he hadn't been nearly toothless. But he still had sharp claws.

Though Iris lived in a shed, her front garden was her pride and joy. Fernley had to go up and mow it every week in summer. 'That push mower was as old as Iris,'

Fernley said. 'Bledy blunt thing. She'd stand over me, making sure I got every clump of grass cut just right. She was right proud of her lawn. That's why she had such a helluva time when the moles came along.'

Now that was a story I remembered hearing in South Molton. It seems that, though that old lady didn't give a toss about living in a shed instead of a house, she went a bit crazy if her nice smooth grass wasn't just right. So what happened was, a bloody mole decided to tunnel under it. Iris was mad as hell. Not just one mole either, but all his sodding cousins and aunts and uncles. So every morning as soon as it was light, old Iris would call her mangy old toothless tabby cat and the two would sit down at the opening of the latest mole tunnel.

'They sat there bleedin' well all day,' Fernley grinned. 'They sure as hell were there every time I cycled up. They didn't move either, while I went about clearing up brambles or whatever job Iris had for me. She had this big ole shovel, must have belonged to her grandad it was so old, and she'd wait with all the patience of a saint, the cat beside her. When one of the little moles poked his twitchy nose out'a the hole, the tabby lifted its paw in warning. Iris would whisper, "There now, kitty, there be another dear'ums coming up," as she bonked the shovel over its head and killed it dead with one blow.'

Fernley guffawed. 'Best mole catcher I knew. She gave me the dead ones to sell for the skins. Made me quite a bit of dosh through old Iris.'

*

That story reminded me of some other old folk who lived on and around Exmoor when I was young. People who would be thought a bit crazy now maybe, but in those days we took folk as they came. We were all just struggling to survive, and any way a person could do it, as long as it did no harm to anyone else, we turned a blind eye.

One of the old ladies was thought to be a witch. But she didn't scare us, though people told stories about her, said she put spells on those who crossed her. She lived in a battered old caravan, surrounded by cages of rabbits. No one knew why she kept all those rabbits. She never sold any, nor did she keep them for eating. They were more like pets. You'd often see her out there feeding the rabbits, talking to them like they were her children.

Anyway, this woman was thought by some to be a witch. She had a rough straw woven basket she carried with her everywhere she went and would pick leaves and flowers from hedgerows and berries from up on the moor. She walked miles and miles every day. She didn't just pick the usual stuff – whortleberries or blackberries, or wild garlic – but all sorts of other weird plants that people said weren't edible. That's why we thought she was a witch. We couldn't think of anything she could do with clumps of gorse flowers and heather and suchlike except to make her witch's potions.

Some people thought she was a healer and went to her for coughs and stomach ailments. She was good with warts especially. If you had them on your hands, all you had to do was let her touch them and they'd be gone next day. I know those who swear it's true, and I have had some experiences with healers myself. Many years ago, I was plastered in warts. I tried some of that blue dye stuff they used in those days to burn them off, but it didn't work. So I talked to a man called Mr Tucker, who said he would bless those warts and they would go away. He looked at them carefully, said some kind words over them, and do you know, they vanished completely not long after. He was a proper healer, he was.

I've known some others too. There was a man who made my ringworm vanish once. And, more recently, I had terrible shingles. They were in my ear, behind my eye, up my nose – I had terrible headaches, they were so bad. It was going on and on; I didn't think the shingles would ever go away. So I rang a man called Pat Piddler. He said to me, 'Tomorrow morning at eight a.m. you think of me. Do that for three mornings in a row, and within a week you'll be better.'

Do you know, it happened just like he said. For three mornings I sat quietly in my garden at eight a.m. thinking about that man, and in less than a week the shingles were gone. That man was another wonderful healer.

This woman in a caravan I was telling you about, though, she had a temper on her. It was all over the village about the time a magpie flew into her open kitchen door one sunny morning and carted off her dinner. There was a local butcher who sometimes had turkey legs for sale. This woman had bought one and it was lying in a saucer on her kitchen counter, waiting to be cooked. She turned her back for a minute to light her stove and, when she turned again, there was this magpie, bold as brass, making off with her turkey leg.

She got it in the end. She had an old air rifle and waited. Sure enough, that magpie came back eventually for more, and she killed it dead. Some people said she ate it, bones and feathers and all, but I never believed that.

You'd think we boys would've played tricks on her, like we did on some others. But the witch never bothered us. If we rampaged behind her caravan playing some game or other, she never complained or called the police. She might get mad as hell at magpies, but never at us. Sometimes she'd even give us stuff, a bowl of blackberries she'd just picked or some windfalls she'd found somewhere. She definitely looked like a witch, mind. Wild grey hair, long skirts with mud on the hems. But she was all right. We mostly left each other alone.

CHAPTER 15

Giant's Blood and Mysterious Footprints

WHEN I WAS A BOY, THERE WERE THE TRAMPS THAT CAME around to the villages every so often. Mother and Father would have them knocking on the door, two or three a year, never the same ones in one year. They all seemed to have long, thin, brown beards streaked with grey and wore long brown overcoats whether it was winter or summer. They were very polite. One man had a beard down to his waist. He had a youngish face but grey hair and this white thin beard tapering down into a point around his belt. He came around once every two or three years. He made a circuit, I believe, walking from one end of Exmoor to another and then back again. He'd knock on the door and ask, in a soft voice, if he could please have a slice of bread and a portion of milk for his tea. He would accept a bit of butter or marge on his bread, but that was all. He wouldn't take another thing, not a scone or a hunk of cheese, not even a coin if it was offered. He'd take his bread and milk and thank us politely then go off. He never slept on anyone's private property but always in some sheltered woodland by a public footpath, or in a tucked-away valley on the moor. Gentlemen of the road, I've heard some folk call them in the old days. That one was a right gentleman, for sure.

A farmer I knew who lives in Cornwall told me about a tramp who used to visit his farm when he was a lad, about sixty years ago now. He was an old fellow with a bushy white beard and a head of hair the same colour and texture as the beard. But the thing the farmer remembers most about him was his size. 'He must've been no more than a couple of inches short of seven foot, would you believe,' he told me. 'A right giant of a man. He'd have been right scary if he weren't gentle as a lamb. All us kids loved him. Mum would give 'im a couple of scones and a mug of tea, and he'd sit outside and eat them. If it were a fine day, me and my sisters gathered around him and he'd tell us stories about the giants that used to roam Cornwall. He had many a tale about them. I think he felt connected, like, because he was surely a giant himself – or at least us kiddies believed so.'

Many years ago, in ancient times, it was believed that giants roamed around the West Country. There's a story about one who was called Cormoran, and he lived around the time of King Arthur, down in Cornwall.

This Cormoran was a nasty piece of work. He hung around St Michael's Mount and spent his days terrorizing people. He stole cattle and dangled them like little souvenirs on loops on his belt, so you can imagine how fierce he was, and how big. Finally, the good folk of Cornwall offered a huge reward to anyone getting rid of this giant. A farmer's son named Jack decided to try for this reward. He dug a huge pit down near a place called Morvah and covered it with straw and sticks and suchlike.

But Jack had a problem. How did he get this giant down off the mount? Then he got a brilliant idea. He started blowing his horn. And blowing, and blowing! That giant got furious. He was trying to sleep, and this sodding horn was keeping him awake. At last he could bear it no longer and went running down towards the sound to shut it up. Sure enough, he fell into the pit Jack had dug and couldn't get out. The story goes that Jack finished him off with a pickaxe and then filled up the pit with earth.

There is a huge stone near Morvah church which is called the Giant's Grave. Some have said that strange groans and other noises have come out from under that stone, especially at night.

Another giant that used to roam about Cornwall frightening the life out of the people was called Bolster. Now this

Bolster, he was a nasty person, and one of the largest giants of them all. He was very brutal to anyone who crossed his path. People were afraid to go out of their houses, it was so bad.

No one knew how to get rid of him. But, luckily, Bolster fell in love. And the person he fell in love with was no other than St Agnes, a very good woman. This Bolster kept pestering Agnes to be his wife, and wouldn't listen when she told him to leave her alone. Finally, she took him to a place near Chapel Porth where there was a hole in the cliffs. She told him that if he filled that hole with blood, she would marry him.

Oh, dearie me, was that giant taken in! He agreed to the scheme, for he was a huge giant and had loads of blood to spare. He figured a couple of gallons would do it, and that was no more than a pinprick for a man that size. But you see, what Bolster didn't know until it was too late was that the hole led to a bottomless pit.

And so he bled to death, and the good folk of Cornwall could come out of their houses again. And if you go to Chapel Porth you'll see the cliffs are still red with the giant's blood.

Stories of giants are everywhere. On the edge of Bodmin Moor there are rows of flat boulders, some over 50 feet around. They are unusual because the larger ones are laid on top of the smaller ones. The tale goes that they were put there during a fierce competition between the giants of Cornwall and the saints.

It started like this. The giants, who ruled much of Cornwall during that time, were getting a bit put out because they thought that the Christian saints, who were starting to grow in number, were having a better time of it. Maybe people were more interested in these new saints than in the old giants. Who knows? The hills and cliffs and valleys were being named after the saints instead of those old giants, and they didn't like it one bit.

The giants got madder and madder and started arguing amongst themselves on how to get rid of the saints. They couldn't come to an agreement, but one of the saints, the smallest of them all, a little tiny fellow called St Tue, came up with an idea. He challenged the leader of the giants, a great strapping bloke called Uther, to a rock-throwing competition. If Uther won, the saints would get out of Cornwall, but if St Tue won, the giants would have to leave.

They all agreed this was a fine idea. Especially the giants, seeing as how Uther was the biggest, strongest, cleverest giant amongst all the giants, and this St Tue was only a tiny sprig of a man. They were laughing and celebrating even before the contest began, sure that their leader would be the winner and that they would have Cornwall all to themselves again, just like they did before all those pesky saints came around.

The day of the contest was cold but bright, with no wind. The saints all gathered around St Tue, and the giants around Uther. Twelve rocks were piled up, all ready for the competition. Uther went first. He took one of the smallest rocks and threw it as far as he could, and oh my, did it go far! It landed way at the top of a nearby hill called Stowes Hill.

The giants were all smirking when St Tue walked over to the stones. But they stopped in a hurry when they saw him pick up one that was much larger than Uther's and hurl it high into the air. What they didn't know, you see, was that the saint had the good Lord's help in the contest.

That rock that St Tue threw landed right on top of Uther's smaller one. The saints cheered and the giants looked stunned. The rock hurling went on for some time. Each go, St Tue chose a larger rock than Uther's, and each one landed right on top of the giant's smaller one.

This went on until the last stone. The two were neck and neck. But when Uther threw his final rock, his strength had gone and he was exhausted. It didn't reach the top of the hill but rolled back down the side to land at St Tue's feet. The saint picked it up and threw it right to the summit of that hill. He'd won the competition – with the help of heaven, of course.

The giants were so impressed that they converted to Christianity on the spot and so were allowed to stay in Cornwall.

What the giants and saints were doing was a game called hurling, which has been played in Cornwall for hundreds of years and is still played there to this day. It is played in teams, with a silver ball. It seems to take many forms, as far as I can see. Sometimes, the players hurl the ball to some goal, like the giants and saints hurled the rocks to the summit of the hill. Sometimes, the game is more like football or rugby, involving scrums and tackles and passes and what have you. I do believe, after the game is over, everyone goes on the razzle. It's a fine old tradition.

In a place called St Cleer there is a line of stone circles which date from 1500 BC. No one knows for sure who put them there, but there's a legend about them, like so many others. In this one, some of the local men were playing hurling on the Sabbath, which just wasn't on. Sunday was a day of rest and churchgoing in those days. St Cleer came along and saw these men playing and got so angry he turned them into the stone circles, doomed to play hurling throughout eternity. It was a fair warning to anyone else who dared play games on a Sunday!

Along with giants and hurlers, Cornwall has many legends about King Arthur, who is said to have lived in Cornwall, in the ruins of a castle on the sea in a village called Tintagel. All around there are stones said to be Arthur's bed, or his stable, or whatever. In St Columb there is a very large stone with marks on it that look like four horseshoe marks. These are believed to be those of King Arthur's horse, left there when the king went riding about the neighbourhood doing his deeds with the other Knights of the Round Table. Near Land's End somewhere is an eight-foot-square block of granite, three foot high, called Table-Men. This is thought to be where many English kings, including King Arthur, used to dine.

*

Talking about the footprints of King Arthur's horse reminds me of some other mysterious footprints. These were in Devon, near the River Exe, and it happened more than a hundred and fifty years ago.

It was winter, and there was a snowfall one night that covered the ground on both sides of the river. The snow was absolutely smooth, with no marks on it except for one strange set of footprints. These weren't deer or horse prints, or any other animal that the villagers could identify. You have to remember that these were country-people, who knew the footprint of every animal and bird in their area. But these were none that anyone had seen before. And the thing that made them wonder, and also get a bit nervous, was that the footprints looked as if they were made by a cloven hoof.

The other odd thing was that the footprints seemed to go through walls and across roofs, and even up drainpipes! Not only that, they went clear across the river, or seemed to, for they went to the edge of the river on one side and started again on the other. The tracks even went right up to the doorways of people's houses then seemed to turn back.

This was such an odd thing that it was even reported in the newspapers. The villagers were sure the prints were those of Satan himself, and that the devil had come in the night looking for sinners. That explained why the footprints went right up to some of the doorways. Everyone was terrified, afraid of leaving their houses.

There was another weird thing about those prints. The

snow that had fallen that night was heavy, and lay very deep. Those footprints went right down to the ground! Many of the locals swore that it was the devil's blazing-hot hooves that had melted the snow so far down.

No explanation has ever been found for those footprints. There were many theories, but they were all discounted. Many animal experts came forward to say no animal or bird could have made tracks like that. Some scientists tried to say the snow might have melted and frozen again in a weird way, but no one could ever prove this. Nor has anything been seen like it since. Since there was no photograph of it, only the testimony of all the villagers and those who came to see the prints, we will never know for sure whether it was the devil or not.

CHAPTER 16

Flights of Fancy

I NOTICED EARLIER THAT THE ROOKS WERE STAYING NEAR TO THEIR nests today. In Devon folklore, that means that it'll rain soon. When the birds fly far away from their rookeries, you know it's meant to be fine.

There are a lot of stories about rooks and their homes, and people used to watch them carefully to see what they were up to. Down Cornwall way, they used to say, if all the rooks leave, someone will die. It worked the other way, though. If the house owner died, the rooks would move away, unless there was someone in the family who would inherit and live on in the property. Once, long ago, a man, a widower with no children, lived in a big old mansion near the sea, all on his own. There'd been a rookery on his land for generations but, when he died, they suddenly all left, just like that! The house stayed empty for years, for some reason, and the rooks never came back. Finally, decades later, the house sold, and the new owners, a young couple with a couple of babies, spent many years doing it up. It wasn't until they'd been there for nearly ten years, and looked like they'd be there for a good ten years more at least, did the rooks finally come back.

I used to think how nice it would be to fly like the birds, but that was before I had a go at it myself.

Now, I've been in some dangerous situations, filming wildlife, climbing trees that were far too tall, or stalking wild creatures like stags in rut or wild boar, and I can tell you, I've been frightened more than once or twice.

But nothing scared me shitless like flying in a microlight.

I went up in this little plane because of Jonathan Marshall. Jon kept birds of prey. I'd know him for a few years, and I'd also seen him at lots of shows, flying his birds. I'd worked with Jonathan on a BBC2 series, on the cliffs of North Devon, and I was impressed at how he knew his birds. He's a good man, very clever.

Jonathan had a Golden Eagle called Samson. He was a beautiful bird, a rescue bird. He'd been born in a cage in a zoo and had never even flown. John raised him up, taught him to perch on his well-protected arm when he whistled. Finally, the time came when John had to let Samson fly away. He let that bird go, and off Samson went. Jonathan wondered if he'd ever see his eagle again. Then he whistled, holding his breath. And would you believe it, that bird flew back right on to his arm! John was that moved, he told me, he cried and cried.

I met Samson up near Bideford on the North Devon coast. John strapped the thick leather gauntlet on my arm to protect it from the eagle's talons. Their talons are enormous, and so powerful. John told me to stand in the field, hold out the arm, with gauntlet, and whistle. Sure enough, within minutes, Samson had flown down and landed on my arm. What an experience that was.

John and the film crew wanted me to go up in this microlight to get footage of the bird in flight. My first reaction was, 'I don't bloody think so.'

I don't like flying, and that's a fact – ever since Julie said to me once, when we were on a plane, 'Isn't it amazing? There's nothing but air under us!' Ever since then, I haven't liked it one bit. When you think about it that way, it puts the fear of God up you. So going up in a tiny micro-light was my idea of hell.

But they talked me into it. A date was made. I was going to go up with a pilot called Lance to try to film this golden eagle.

I worked myself up into a sweat before that date. I had to keep getting my nerve up, telling myself it'd be fine. But then the flight was cancelled. The weather was bad. Do you know, I didn't know whether to thank the good Lord or to sit down and cry. It was wonderful not to be going up in the air that day, but I knew I'd have to start all over again, getting my nerve up.

Would you believe, this happened four times. I'd work like hell to get my courage up, and then the day would come and the flight would be cancelled.

So when the weather finally changed and we were able to get up, I was a right bag of nerves. You can imagine what I was feeling, going up and down like that. One minute we were taking off, the next it was all off.

But, on this day, the weather was fine. There was some worry that the eagle would not be able to fly high enough to go alongside us, but I had other worries. I was watching that microlight come in to land and it looked no bigger than a little bird against that big blue sky.

It landed not far from where we were waiting. When I saw it, my heart jumped and my knees were knocking like drums. It was the smallest thing I'd ever seen. It looked more like a big kite or something with an engine underneath than a plane. I was supposed to go up in that? Bloody hell, this was going to be all my worst nightmares come at once.

Right, I thought, looking at that flimsy flying machine. I knew what my first job would be: to sneak a miniature bottle of whiskey in my pocket when no one was looking.

And that's exactly what I did. It made me feel a bit more secure, though my heart was still pounding away. I tapped the small bottle in my pocket to give me courage and walked up to the microlight.

Lance handed me a helmet and a flying suit, which I put

on. I got my camera, and then there was nothing else to do but get in that plane and get ready for take-off.

Can you imagine how I felt? I can't begin to tell you how terrified I was.

Lance revved up and started down the field. It scared the shit out of me. The plane was shaking away and I thought it was coming apart.

We didn't take off. We got to the end of the field, but the take-off failed to happen. Lance had to try again. I was shaking like hell. Down the field we went for a second time, and this time we took off.

We were up in the air, and I felt like I was flying like a bird as we went towards the sea. I might even have stopped shaking if the plane hadn't dropped suddenly out of the sky. That's what it seemed like to me. I yelled at Lance, 'What the hell was that?'

'No problem, just an air pocket,' he said.

I reached for my whiskey bottle. My heart nearly stopped again. I couldn't get at it, because I had on that sodding flying suit. The whiskey was in my other trousers. *Shit*, I thought. What a blow that was.

We were up there for about an hour. I can't say I ever got to love it, even with the green fields, the dark-blue sea down there to look at. I'd rather see it all standing on my own two feet on earth.

But I'm glad I did it. I got some good shots of that golden eagle. It was difficult, though, leaning out and twisting in all directions trying to film the bird. In the meantime, there was a camera attached to the wing of the microlight so that I was filmed filming the bird. This episode was shown as part of the BBC series I did. I'm happy to say that camera didn't show us tumbling down from the sky, as I was sure we were going to do when Lance said it was time to begin landing. We started to turn over to go down, and I thought my eyes must have turned inside out. I was sure we'd crash. My heart was in my mouth. We came in fast and hit the ground hard. I thought all my bones were breaking.

As we pulled to a stop, Jonathan ran up to the micro-light. 'Are you all right, Johnny?' he asked.

'Yes,' I said. 'But what an experience that was. I can't say I'd like to do it all over again.'

Then I told him about the whiskey bottle. 'I couldn't get the bloody thing out of my pocket,' I said. Jonathan laughed like hell and, when I stopped trembling, I laughed with him.

I was so pleased that I'd gone up there, though. Everyone knew how scared I'd been, and they kept saying, 'Well done, Johnny,' which pleased me too.

I think Julie was glad to have me down. She knew about my fears, and I know she had a few of her own when she saw how small the plane was. 'You never know what things can go wrong,' she said to me when I was safe down. 'I was as worried as you were, Johnny.'

CHAPTER 17

A Famous Highwayman

THESE DAYS, SPRINGTIME BRINGS A RUSH OF WORK FOR ME, AS IT does for everyone living in the country, from farmers getting their ground ready for sowing to the shopkeepers and publicans and café owners and B&B people getting ready for the tourist season.

There's a lot to do on our land, for a start. Clearing up after winter, seeing to the bird-boxes, the badger's wheel that I made to entice the animals to our place. Clearing out dead leaves and branches from the pond. Getting ready for all the new growth, the new nests and eggs and little creatures.

There's so much to photograph too. Films to make. Long days when the light is good. I spend hours up on the moor or on our land, waiting and watching. It's an amazing time, springtime.

My Exmoor safaris start in spring too. I do about four a week, more in the summer. I take four people at a time, either on a morning safari or an afternoon one. I get folk from all over the world come on my safaris, and I've met some nice people. Many of them come back again and again. One man from Taunton, he's called John too, comes down to see me every year with his wife. He makes walking sticks and, each time he comes, he brings me one. I've had all sorts, each with a different top on it. I've had fox heads, duck heads and a badger head, all on top of these walking sticks.

Also, a man called Andrew came down with his whole family on safari, but this time he brought something very, very different. He said, 'I've got something better than a walking stick, Johnny. You wait until lunchtime.'

In those days, I had the time to stop for a pub lunch after the safaris, so that is what we did. First, though, we had a look at Tarr Steps. Now that's a truly wonderful beauty spot on Exmoor. The stone steps that go over the River Barle are very old, maybe from around the thirteenth century. Some say that the steps date back to 1000 BC. It's what they call a clapper bridge. There are seventeen huge slabs of flat stone, some weighing up to five tons, making a bridge across the water. Alongside the river on both sides are beautiful woodland walks, filled with majestic old oak trees, as well as beech and ash and hazel. It's a brilliant spot for the wildlife. The river is filled with salmon and trout, and there are otters too. If you're lucky you might see a hawk or kestrel.

The story goes that the devil built Tarr Steps, after a giant had challenged him to a competition. The devil got very possessive of his stone bridge and wouldn't let anyone cross it, on pain of death. To test out whether the devil really meant this, they put a cat on the bridge. The poor creature got to the middle and dropped down dead, so folk knew the devil's threats were to be taken seriously.

Finally, one night, a brave local parson met the devil on the bridge and stood up to him. 'Look 'ere,' said the parson. 'I've got the good Lord on my side. You've got to let folk cross.'

Such was the power of the parson, or the Lord, that the devil relented. Just a tad, though. People could cross, but not when the devil was sunning himself on the stone slabs of the bridge. So be warned, my good readers – if you find yourself at Tarr Steps and want to cross over the bridge, make sure you don't do it if you see a strange, fiery figure with a pointy tail and horns lounging about enjoying the summer sunshine. Wait till he's gone, just to be on the safe side!

As I was saying, after one of these morning safaris, we stopped for a pub lunch. My wife Julie was meeting us at The Stag's Head in Filleigh. We were seated already, but this Andrew I was telling about rushed up to greet her. He'd met her before, on other safaris. After she'd ordered some food, Andrew said, 'Johnny, I've got something special for you here. I wanted to wait until your fine wife got here before giving it to you, for this is something I've made especially for you.'

I told him I didn't expect any presents, but he wouldn't take no for an answer. He got out this huge box he'd been lugging about with him. He'd asked me to stow it in the jeep when we got going but wouldn't tell me what it was. Now he was beaming at me, pointing at this enormous box. 'Open it, Johnny,' he said.

I opened it up, and there staring me right in the face was this great big wooden owl. It was so lifelike I had a fright for a second or two, thinking he had a bloody live owl in that box, and a monster one at that, it was so huge. It was at least two feet wide and three feet high.

It was a big thing, that owl. This man Andrew had carved it with a chainsaw, of all things.

It was a lovely present, and I thanked him sincerely for it.

I had to get on with the safari, so Julie took the owl back home. She had this tiny car, a little Corsa, and the only place for that big old owl was in the front passenger seat. Julie had to strap it in to keep it from falling over.

All the way home, people were staring at that owl. It looked so real, except for its huge size, that one or two drivers nearly rammed into Julie's car, they were gaping that hard. She had to go through South Molton to pick up some groceries on the way and collected quite a crowd in the car park. 'I didn't think I'd make it home with that owl,' Julie grinned at me later when I got back. 'You should have seen the stares I got as I drove through town.'

The funny thing was, a few days later someone I knew said he'd heard that a story was going around town about a great big tawny owl spotted by several people, bigger than any other owl seen in these parts.

Julie and I had a good laugh at this. Stories get around and breed like rabbits, getting bigger all the time and making more tales as they go around. A good thing too. Where would any of us be without the stories folk tell?

It was a grand present, that owl. I still don't know how that man carved it with his chainsaw.

It was a perfect evening as I was going home that day, pretty as a picture. I walked on a bit to Landacre Bridge, another beautiful spot. It's a fine stone bridge, the oldest arched bridge on Exmoor. It was made famous in *Lorna Doone*. The highwayman Tom Faggus, one of the characters in the book, escapes over Landacre Bridge after one of his escapades. It must have been wild country in those days, the 1600s, when the book was set. The river and that old bridge, and the Barle Valley, all hills and slopes and hidden valleys. That's all still there, but many of the fields are grassy, cultivated. There're still wooded areas, and plenty of beech hedges. Wildflowers are coming out everywhere now, in fields and woods and meadows. The primroses have been out for ages, and now it's the bluebells.

Lorna Doone came out in the late 1800s, but quite a few folk say that the tales of Tom Faggus were around long before then. There are still stories of that highwayman around today. He had a horse called Winnie, a strawberry mare that was as famous as Tom for her courage and wildness. In one story, the law officers got wind of the fact that Tom was in an alehouse in Simonsbath and surrounded the place. Tom, being an alert bugger even when on the ale, knew something was up. He let out a shrill whistle that nearly broke the eardrums of everyone in the crowded pub. Winnie, his mare, heard it from the stables outside, where she was locked in. Breaking down the stable door, she rushed to the alehouse, knocked down a few of the law officers with her hooves and came to Tom's rescue. As the crowd scattered in front of the wild horse, Tom leaped out, jumped on Winnie, and they galloped away to safety.

I've heard tell of this story taking place in Porlock as well as Simonsbath. Either that highwayman and his horse escaped from more than one inn on Exmoor, or else it's too good a story not to be claimed by more than one town.

According to the old stories, Tom Faggus was a North Molton lad. He was a blacksmith, but also owned a bit of land, and had the right of common up on the moor for more than two hundred sheep and other beasts. He was a clever chap, because he could read and write, in a time when many folk couldn't.

Tom was mad about a girl from South Molton called Betsy Paramore. She was a pretty little maid and crazy about Tom too. They planned to get married, and the wedding was coming up soon, but something happened to change their plans. Tom got mixed up in some kind of lawsuit with a wealthy country gentleman and lost every penny he had. In those days, you couldn't marry without money, so poor Tom couldn't have his girl. He was so angry and bitter about it that he became a highwayman. He wasn't the nasty kind, though, no way. He might have robbed the rich of all they had, every jewel and valuable trinket and cash, but he never hurt anyone and he never took from the poor. And he never ever said a rude thing to any woman but treated them all like the gentleman he was.

That didn't stop the law from trying to get Tom Faggus. The rich gentry and suchlike were fed up with losing their goods to Tom, for he was very successful in being a high-wayman. Determined to get rid of him once and for all, a group of men took their firearms and rode out to find him. Tom heard about it but instead of hiding out, he rode out on his horse, Winnie, to meet them. He put on his finest clothes and tucked a Bible in his pocket, but stick-ing out for the men to see. None of them recognized the highwayman!

Tom asked if he could help the gentlemen in any way, and they explained what they were up to. They were going to get that Tom Faggus, dead or alive! Tom nodded and asked if their guns were in good condition, for it was very damp that time of year. He suggested they fired up in the air and then reloaded, to make sure their firearms were ready to be fired the minute they spotted the highwayman. Thinking this was a fine idea, and thanking the man who suggested it, they all discharged their guns into the air. At that point, Tom pulled his own pistol and told them who he was. While they stared, frightened to death at this man they'd heard was so ruthless, Tom took all their money and gave it to all the poor village folk who'd gathered around watching the fun. Then he rode off and was way out of sight before the men could reload and go after him. They never did get him. He was some fellow, that Tom Faggus.

CHAPTER 18

A Kind and Loving Spirit

IT WAS A LOVELY DAY, THAT DAY I STOOD THERE NEAR LANDACRE Bridge watching the sunlight on a steep green hill that sloped right down to the river. The lambs were grouping themselves, as they do, for play, and started running and jumping up and down the fields. About a dozen there were, all leaping together. The ewes just chewed their cud, enjoying the warmth.

All those sheep reminded me of some of the wonderful sheep fairs I went to as a boy, in South Molton. Farmers brought in their sheep for miles around, to be sold to the highest bidder.

It was a big day out, not just for the farmers but for their whole families. And for all us lot too, anyone living anywhere near the town. Tents were set up on the edges of the big sheep fields with people inside selling pasties and tea and cakes, and maybe some home-made stuff like knitted tea cosies and other such odds and sods.

There was a fairground for us kids, with rides and sideshows. Some of those rides were rough, looking back. There was something we called the whirly-ride, or near enough, which was a switchback thing, a wooden circle going round and round. There were hard wooden seats on it. The thing went around on a narrow angle so you were thrown about at the risk of a broken neck, it went so fast. They were all pretty damn basic, those rides, back along in those days. There was one with bucket seats on the edge of a long chain. They swung around and around, so fast it's a wonder those chains didn't break. I think they did, now and again. Those old fairgrounds weren't the safest in the world, but we kids loved them.

Then there were all those sideshows. You'd throw wooden balls at coconuts, or darts on numbers on a board on the ground. And those goldfish. All the fairs had goldfish in these small bowls, all lined up in a row. For a sixpence you got three little plastic balls. You had to try to get them into the goldfish bowls – a lot harder task than it looked. If you got one in, which wasn't often, you got to take the goldfish home in a bowl. It was a big thing, then, taking home a goldfish in a bowl.

Later, when my boys were growing up, the fairground people got wise. If you got a ball in one of the bowls, they took the fish out and put it in a plastic bag filled with water. Many a poor fish died before you could get it home.

The best thing for us lads was the shooting ranges. There were rows of metal animals, about two or three inches high, for us to try to hit with an air rifle. They were moving on a conveyor belt, so that made it harder. The animals were tigers and lions and giraffes and hippopotamuses – all sorts. You were supposed to think you were in Africa on safari.

There was always noise at the sheep fairs. All day long there was the baaing of animals in the pens as they were bought and sold and moved about. There was the tinny music of the fairground, coming from the carousel, or other rides. There would be a local band somewhere, giving a show. And of course the shouts and hollers of the farmers, and us kids shrieking and yelling.

The pubs did the best business, though, at those sheep fairs. The day before, all the pub owners rolled up their good mats or rugs and put them away. They left the floors bare, mostly, or put out their old tattered mats. Some of the pubs had sawdust sprinkled on the floor, on those market days. The farmers came in with their boots caked in mud after a day out in the sheep fields. The pubs were crammed half the night with the locals and the farmers from out of town drinking cider, playing dominoes and shove ha'penny.

It was a big day for the town, the South Molton sheep fair.

*

Carnival time was another great holiday for us. 'I used to love the carnivals,' Julie said to me when we were talking about the fun we used to have. 'I remember when I was about twelve or thirteen and wanted to be the crown bearer for the Carnival Princess. Do you remember my mum and Aunt Ella, what they did to make my wish come true?'

I didn't know Julie then, but I know the story. I loved Julie's mum, and so did her grandchildren. My grand-daughter Roxy, when she was a young teenager and had her first boyfriend, asked her gran how to kiss a boy. 'Just imagine you are sucking an orange,' said her gran, 'and if you find you like it, suck some more.'

That was Julie's mum for you. Full of fun and good humour. Her name was Dot and she was the youngest of ten children. The family moved fourteen times as Dot was growing up, but it didn't seem to harm her at all. She was strong and healthy, walked everywhere as a child. Later, when Dot was married, she went everywhere on her bicycle, and so did her great friend, Julie's Aunt Ella. They would meet up in South Molton whenever they could. Ella would bring Dot some of her elderberry wine to take home. She made the best elderberry wine in Devon.

At one time, they had only one bike between them. Dot would pedal over to Aunt Ella's house in Great Heal, a few miles up the road, and if it was her turn for the bike, Dot would walk home, leaving the bike at Aunt Ella's.

Ella used to take Julie for bike rides when she was little.

The buzzard is a beautiful bird: large
and powerful, but fast and graceful.
Watching it fly is something else.

I'd been trying to get a picture of this cuckoo for ages. I could always hear him out there – cuckoo, cuckoo – like he was mocking me. Then one day, when I was with my friend Fred, the darned cuckoo flew straight out of a hawthorn tree right in front of us. Thank goodness I had my camera ready!

Left: It always gladdens me to hear birdsong, especially when all that business of nest-making is going on in springtime. The sparrows are chittering away, the thrushes and blackbirds are singing louder than ever, and the woodpeckers are tap-tap-tapping on the trees.

Above: There's a lovely story about why the kingfisher is so beautifully coloured. When Noah built his ark, the kingfisher's feathers were all grey and colourless but when the rains finally stopped, the bird was so happy to be free that he flew straight up to heaven where some blue sky rubbed off on him and the sun's golden glow stained his chest.

Left: I lost all my blue tits in the heat last spring and it broke my heart. There were nine eggs in the nest but even though seven of them hatched, all lively and sprightly things, within twenty-four hours they were all gone.

Below: You can see why folk in olden times were frightened of barn owls; they can look particularly spooky. They even used to be known as ghost owls because of their white faces and great white wings.

Left: It was a lucky day for me when I got this picture. Out of nowhere, two long ears poked out from behind a hawthorn bush. Then, to my surprise, this plucky hare jumped out towards me, not away, before tearing off on his great big, thumping back legs.

Below: If a badger crosses your path, it's meant to mean good luck. But there's a catch. If the animal drags its feet a bit as he walks along in front of you, and happens to scratch up a bit of dirt – oh dearie me, you'd better start getting your coffin ready.

Above: We always see some ponies on my safaris. They're as pretty as a picture, these animals, but the Exmoor pony is a tough creature. Living on the moor needs a great deal of stamina and requires a good weatherproof coat to survive the harsh winters.

Below: I hid myself in a hedge to get this picture of these playful fox cubs. They'd made their den in the middle of a steep field and I stayed there all afternoon keeping an eye on it, watching the cubs go in and out. They didn't go far, though. Not yet.

Above and below: The deer that roam Exmoor are wonderful creatures. Long ago, in ancient times, the stag was considered to be one of the gods of the woodland and thought to bring good things to whoever saw it. Maybe it was because of those huge antlers.

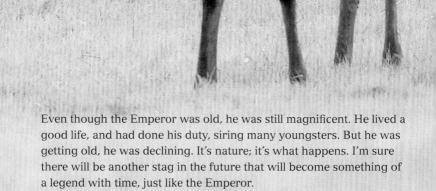

Even though the Emperor was old, he was still magnificent. He lived a good life, and had done his duty, siring many youngsters. But he was getting old, he was declining. It's nature; it's what happens. I'm sure there will be another stag in the future that will become something of a legend with time, just like the Emperor.

She'd be sat on the seat and Aunt Ella would pedal standing up. There were no brakes on that bike. Whoever was cycling had to dive into a hedgerow to stop the thing.

'It reminds me of that bike I had once,' I said to Julie as we were laughing over that story. 'All it was was a bloody steel frame and a chain. No tyres or tubes, no brakes, nothing. Rode it till it fell apart, with me on it.'

Anyway, it was during carnival time that Dot and Aunt Ella got together with a fine plan, to help Julie get to be crown bearer. Whoever sold the most carnival tickets got the job. Tickets were a penny each and, of course, all the families of the young girls who wanted the job were out selling those tickets day and night. Dot and Ella were too, but with a difference. They got hold of a rubber doll wearing a red and blue kilt. Every time someone bought a ticket, they were allowed to put their penny in this doll, and every time a penny went in, the kilt went up. This caused so much hilarity that everyone bought tickets, and Julie got to be crown bearer.

There were so many markets in those first years that Julie and I were together. Great celebrations they were, with the heavy old cart horses plodding the streets, livestock everywhere, the local bobby walking the beat and having time to stop in the pub now and again. Julie and I used to meet all our friends at the King's Arms then. Everyone we knew was there, feeling happy, joining in the fun.

Julie's mum Dot was a wonderful woman, like my own mother. The two women got on well together. Everyone called them Perky and Pinky. In another book, I've told how I had to work to get Julie's family to accept me. I wasn't exactly what every man dreamed about for his daughter at that time, what with being a poacher as well as a bit wild in my young days.

But my family liked Julie from the start, even though, the first time she had Sunday dinner with us, she broke the handle of Mum's best china cup. She was helping with the washing-up, doing all the right things, and crash! The cup fell right out of her hands and landed on the lino.

Julie felt terrible, as you can imagine. But my mum liked her anyway, and they got on fine until the day Mum died.

Dot lived to the good age of eighty-six. I've said how they moved fourteen times in all, but what I didn't say was that this was all in around the same place she was born, in Exmouth. Her family owned a newsagent's there, and Julie used to come out early every morning to deliver the newspapers.

When she married Julie's father, who was a farmer's son from Twichen, who later became a butcher, he took her to a cottage in Sheridan, in the middle of nowhere. There was no water there, and no electricity, and Exmouth was a good forty, fifty miles away. She was such a town girl that the first time she went out on the land she wore high-heeled shoes.

She soon got used to her new life, though. Like I said, she learned to ride a bike and went everywhere on it. Even when she was old she was young at heart. She loved music and dancing and, later, all her grandchildren. They loved her too. Roxy is one of my grandchildren, as I believe I've mentioned before, and she still feels close to Julie's mum. Roxy still talks to her, and feels that her gran's spirit is still around, looking after her.

Julie does too. She feels comforted knowing her mum is around, even though she passed away years ago. Once, a few years back, Julie got very upset when she couldn't find some cash she had put away in the house. In those days, we'd put our market takings in this cream container, and there was £240 in it. We needed the money for something, but the container was gone. Julie looked everywhere and couldn't find it. She'd just about given up hope of ever seeing the money again when she sat down, feeling her mum near her. 'Mum, where could it be?' she silently asked her.

Julie felt as if her mum was taking her back into the kitchen, where she'd looked a dozen times. Hardly know-ing what she was doing, she shoved her hand way back between the kitchen units, and there it was, the container with the money. Julie had never thought to look there. 'If I hadn't asked my mum, it'd probably still be there,' she said to me later.

It's wonderful, to feel like this. That you're being watched over by those you love who have passed on.

Roxy also likes to tell the story about a white feather floating down in our garden. I had a cross that was very special to me that was given to me by the wife of my best mate in the army. Brian and his wife, Maureen, were great friends of ours for years, and Brian and I had been sent out to Hong Kong together. Maureen gave me a wonderful present once, this beautiful silver cross. It was a special gift, and I was glad of it.

Unfortunately, I lost that cross. I looked everywhere but couldn't find it. Julie looked too, but it was no use. It looked like that cross was gone for good.

Weeks later, Roxy and Louise, still little kids, were sitting in the garden when Roxy saw a white dove's feather fluttering to the ground. She watched it come slowly, out of nowhere it seemed like. It fell to the grass on the lawn and Roxy put her hand out to pick it up, for it was a beautiful thing. She got the surprise of her life when, underneath the feather, was my lost cross! To this day, Roxy is sure that feather was guiding her to it. She knew how upset I was about losing it.

I'm always getting letters from people who have read my other books and know about my beliefs. They tell me of their own similar experiences. I don't have the time to answer them back but I am always grateful that they've taken the time to write.

CHAPTER 19

Standing Stones

I HEARD A FUNNY STORY FROM AN OLD FARMER UP DARTMOOR way. He was having a hard time making a living from his small patch of rough old ground and, even though he had grazing rights on the moor, it was still hard going. So one day he and his missus decided to rent a couple of rooms out for the B&B business. They had a big old farmhouse and the children were all left home so there was plenty of room.

Now, you've got to remember that this was in the days before the big boom in tourism in the West Country. The B&Bs were in farmhouses, but not smart like they mostly are now. The guests had to live in with the family and share a bathroom with other guests, or even with the family themselves.

This couple – Jenny and Rod they were called – had the only guesthouse in their small Dartmoor village, and Rod admitted it was pretty rough. '"Basic", we called it in our advertisements,' Rod said later with a devilish grin. 'Hot water only in the evening for two hours, a tarnished brass bed with a lumpy mattress, and hot-water bottles for heating. But I'll tell you this – the wife used to cook up the best breakfast on Dartmoor. Three eggs fresh from our hens, local bacon and sausages, scones fresh out of the old Aga with a girt dollop of Jenny's clotted cream made straight from our milking cow the night before.'

Rod tells the story of two guests who got tangled up with some of the ghosts that are said to haunt the moor. 'They didn't run across the black hen, did they?' I asked with a chuckle. 'Maybe they gathered some black eggs for their breakfast.'

'No,' Rod said, 'this here weren't no animal spirits. I'll tell 'ee what happened.'

And so he did, telling me all about the old legend of the Nine Maidens, a standing-stone circle not far from the village of Belstone.

The circle, sometimes called the Nine Virgins, is not very wide. The stones are small, about thigh high, and the tale goes like this. Those stones are really nine maidens from the village who danced on the Sabbath and so were turned to stone for their sins. Poor maids – what a harsh punishment for a bit of dancing! So the only bit of fun those ladies have now is once a year, on the summer solstice, just before dawn, when mysterious things are supposed to happen. They turn from stones into women again and dance for a very short time before they're turned back to stone. They dance naked as the day they were born, the reason being that stones don't have clothes and theirs were torn off when they were changed.

Now, like all legends told about Exmoor and Dartmoor, there are different variations on this tale, but this is the one I heard from Rod, and this is the one Rod told to a young couple that was staying at his farmhouse B&B during one solstice, about thirty, forty years ago. The guests were intrigued by the story. They decided they'd spend the night at the stone circle to see what was up. Mind, they didn't really believe they'd see any ghosts, being modern young folk and not in the least superstitious.

Well, what a shock they had that night. They were lucky, for it was clear and moonlit, and the ground was dry after a good spell without rain. They'd brought blankets and a bit of whiskey in a flask to keep themselves warm in case the night got chilly. Of course, they were young and their hormones were raging, so they had a bit of fun to keep warm as well, if you know what I mean. All that exertion, not to mention the alcohol, tired them out, though, so they couldn't keep awake. When the light started to break over the rocky outcrops of Dartmoor, they were sound asleep.

Some kind of weird music woke them up, like they told Rod later. The first thing they saw was a woman playing a kind of long pipe instrument. It was early dawn, but still fairly dark, yet light enough to see the woman was stark naked. So were the other women they noticed next, all dancing starkers around the stone circle.

None of them appeared to notice the couple now trying to hide behind some of the stones. They were too busy dancing. The bloke was too terrified to give the women more than a shocked look before grabbing his girl by the hand and running away with her as fast as their legs could carry them. Off they flew, back to where they left their car at the edge of the moor. The funny thing was that they were stark bollocks naked too, having stripped off their clothes in the fun and games of the night before and were sleeping with only a couple of blankets for warmth. But they were too terrified to even pick up their clothes and had to drive back to the farmhouse just as nature had made them.

Good job it was that it was only just past four in the morning and no one saw them. Jenny and Rod woke up when they heard them come in, and they all sat about drinking pots of tea for hours, after the young chap and his girlfriend got over the embarrassment of having to get out of the car without any clothes on. They were convinced that they'd seen the ghosts of those nine maidens and, now that their fright was over, they were full of it. Couldn't wait to get back up country to tell their mates. 'They looked so human, so real, just like you and me,' they kept saying over and over again.

Rod and Jenny kept pouring tea and listening, and when those two finally headed for home, they had a right laugh. They knew good and well that, once or twice at the summer solstice, this being the old hippie days, a few women gathered at the stone circle to dance naked in honour of the legend of the nine maidens.

'But we weren't about to tell 'em,' Rod said later. 'They be much happier thinking they'd seen ghosts.'

In Cornwall, there's a similar story about a stone circle. In Boleigh, near Land's End, there is a large circle of nineteen stones called the Merry Maidens. This is bigger than the Dartmoor stone circle I was telling you about, but the legend has the same sort of warning to it. In this one, the nineteen maidens were on their way to a church service. But on their way, they heard music. They wandered over to a nearby field to hear where it was coming from. There they saw two pipers, handsome young men, I reckon, for off they went into the field, all nineteen of these girls, dancing like crazy, having one helluva time.

Suddenly, a storm came up – like in about a couple of seconds, so you knew this wasn't any old storm. A thunderclap louder than was ever heard around those parts came crashing out of the sky, and all those lovely young maidens, and the two pipers, were turned to stone.

It was a punishment for dancing on the Sabbath.

Not far from that stone circle, there are two tall standing stones. These are the two pipers who led those girls astray.

*

So, those are just a couple of the old stories about people turned into stones, but there are many others, too many to be told here. There are even stories about great stones that come alive at night and wander the countryside.

There's a stone like that in Somerset. It's perched on a hillside at Shipham. This is some big stone, let me tell you. It's called the Wimblestone, and you can see it there in the daylight, looking like an ordinary stone.

But, at night, the Wimblestone moves. It doesn't just move a little bit, it goes wandering all over the country-side. Farmworkers in the past, going home late at night, have it lurking behind hedgerows, making the earth tremble as it rolled along the ground. It scared them half to death, this great dark shape coming towards them, making odd noises in the night.

It never hurt anyone, though. It seems a sociable kind of stone. The legend goes that it used to visit another stone in the vicinity, called the Waterstone, maybe stopping off for a drink or two with its friend – I don't know!

I haven't heard of anyone seeing the stone lately, but it's said that the Wimblestone can still be seen when there is a full moon on Midsummer's Eve. The stone has a high old time that night. It goes out dancing in the field. Anyone passing by at that time can see something fantastic. It's a glimmer of the gold that is hidden under the Wimblestone. It shines and glitters and is very tempting, folk say.

But don't try to go grab a nugget or two. That stone

doesn't like anyone who tries to steal his gold. That's the only time it might be dangerous, if you go too near its treasure.

CHAPTER 20

The Parson and the Clerk

ROXY WAS OVER AT MY HOUSE EARLIER TODAY, AND I WAS
telling her some more of the stories I remember from long
ago. Roxy and Louise are first cousins and get along like
two sisters. Roxy's twenty now as I write this, and she's
taken over the work of organizing my safaris, making
appointments, talking to interested people on the phone,
and leaving me free to get on with my work.

We were in the garden, talking about the baby deer we
raised there, Bambi. It lived in our back garden for twelve
years, and I wrote a book about her. She had been found
hanging by the leg from a pig-wire fence, badly injured.
After a serious operation to amputate her damaged leg,
she came to live with us. That three-legged creature was
very important in our lives, and we were all sad when she

finally died. 'But Bambi had a good life here, Grandad,' Roxy said.

'You're right, Roxy. It's a wonder she lived at all.'

I said to Roxy that she'll have good stories to pass on to her children, about that deer. She said, 'Not only about Bambi. About you. I'll never forget driving across the moor with you and you kept asking me, "What's that herb over there?" I always forgot – I was only a little kid – so you told me over and over again, trying to drum it into my head. And then next time I'd forget it. Finally, one day, you asked me, and I said, quick as a flash, "Rosebay willowherb." You should have seen the look on your face! You were so surprised that finally I'd remembered that it was ages before you asked me about anything else. You couldn't even think of another question.'

Julie had just come in, and we had a good laugh about that. Roxy went on, 'I learned so much about animals and plants from you, Grandad. You were always pointing out things to me. You still do.'

Julie said, 'Remember that hare you two found? You must have been about eight or nine at the time, Roxy.'

'I remember. We were taking some people out to Grandad's old hide, to see some badgers, and we spotted this hare in some bushes, not looking very good. Grandad and I caught it. It was covered with ticks, so he brought it home and the two of us picked off all the ticks, kept it until it had gained back its strength.'

'It was a sweet little thing,' Julie said.

'I called it Thistle. Grandad and I were always rescuing things, birds and little animals.'

'And you were always frightening the hell out'a me, Roxy, when you were little.' I grinned at her. 'I never knew what you'd pick up. D'you remember when you leaned out the window of my truck and handed me a big bunch of leaves and flowers? "This is for you, Grandad," you said, and tried to push them into my face for a smell of them.'

'Did you jump!' Roxy laughed. 'You hollered, "Are you trying to poison me?" and then grabbed the stuff, threw it out the window.'

'It was ragwort. The most poisonous plant on Exmoor. More'n one animal has died of it, and there you were shoving them in my face.'

I loved having my granddaughters riding with me when they were little, helping them learn about this wonderful place they lived in. Roxy, when she was older, tried to spot deer before I did, and got pretty good at it.

I remember when I first showed them the lilies near Molland, at a place called Sheepwash Hill. It's a fine place, out in the countryside, and it's at its best in May when the Sheepwash Lily comes out. The way up to Sheepwash Hill is a pretty one. It's a wooded road lined with beech, ash, hazel, evergreens, with the odd farm or house tucked away behind. Campion and other wildflowers grow everywhere this time of year.

The lily grows wild on Sheepwash Hill here, and in May it is pretty as a picture. Now, the long name for this flower is either Lilium Pyrenaicum, or maybe the other way around, Pyrenaicum Lilium – I never can remember – but we hereabouts call it the Sheepwash Lily. It only grows for a short time and only on Exmoor, and a fine sight it is too. It's yellow and red and the leaves are curled back more than a true lily leaf.

There's a story about the origins of this flower. It's said that some medieval monks from Spain brought the bulbs over here. Apparently, the monks had a rest home somewhere outside of Molland, or so the tale goes. Though I've also heard tell that it was long-ago soldiers, coming from Spain, who carried the seeds with them in their kit bags, or whatever they called them in those days. Monks or soldiers, both stories say the seeds came from Spain, and it's true they only grow here in this place.

There was a fog the other night that was so thick I nearly missed my turning for home, though I know the roads around here like the back of my hand. I was at the coast, and the mist was rolling off the sea. There's so much coastline in the West Country, and all so different. There are long sandy beaches and craggy cliffs and huge rock formations, and everything in between.

I was reminded of a story about one of these rock formations at a place in Devon called Dawlish that is not that far from Exeter. It seems that a century or so ago, or thereabouts, the Bishop of Exeter took sick. He was quite poorly, and one of the local parsons started to visit him often. Now, this might sound like a good thing, but this particular parson did not do it out of kindness. There were many ill folk in his own parish, but he ignored them, spending every free minute visiting the bishop. You see, this man was very ambitious, and had dreams of becoming bishop himself. That was the only reason he kept visiting. I think he lived in hope that either the bishop would reward him if he survived or, if not, the parson would be in line to get the job.

The parson had a servant, a clerk, who went with him on his visits, to help find the way and, in general, to make the journey easier. One evening, a terrible fog came on them as they set off for the bishop's house, and the clerk got lost in all those narrow cobbled streets. They wandered this way and that until they were completely lost.

The parson was in a fury, terrified that some other young keen vicar or other such parson would be visiting the bishop at that very moment and taking his place as the main comforter of the bishop.

The parson got into such a temper that he shouted at his clerk, 'The devil would make a better guide than you are.'

Oh dearie me, not a wise thing to say, as you shall see. Along came a farmer down the road, and the parson asked for directions. The farmer said he didn't exactly know where the bishop lived but, since it was late, and a very nasty night, he would guide them to a safe house where they could spend the night and continue their journey in the morning after a good breakfast.

This is what they did, and indeed they got a good meal that night and slept in a decent bed. But in the morning, when they woke up, the house was gone and they were lying down on a hard, rocky place. They were trapped on a rock in the middle of the sea, their horses far away on shore. As they sat pondering what to do, the farmer appeared, who turned out not to be a farmer at all but the devil. 'Well, you said I'd make a better guide,' the devil cried, and he tossed the two into the sea and turned them into stone. The two rocks are still there, called the Parson and the Clerk.

Later on that evening, we were all working on the land. All the family help out: Craig and Stuart, my sons, and everyone who has some time to spare. All the bluebells were out, and the woods were full of them. Earlier in the year, it was white with snowdrops and then yellow with wild daffodils. Craig was cutting up wood for winter fires and Stuart was hacking off some dead branches in the woods. Roxy's boyfriend, Billy, was building up an old stone well that had crumbled. The well was many years old, made of slate and stone, and long out of use. Billy was fixing it up, restoring it, and it was looking good.

Julie was looking at a special tree planted in the field. It came from a conker tree in Paris, round about ten years ago, when we brought some conkers back home for Louise, only a kid herself then, who planted them in a couple of pots in the garden. Two out of the three grew, and those we took over to the land. One took, and it's there now, covered with new leaves and white blossom.

There are many things on our land that are special to us. There's an oak tree with names carved on it, a rope swing on it. All these things remind us of the fun we've had here when the kids were growing up. And the fun we're still having.

There are always surprises, too. I had one that evening, when I went to the pond to see our Canadian geese. I crept up all quiet like, so as not to disturb the parents. They had laid five eggs in a rough nest they'd built on the island of the pond and, three days ago, the eggs had hatched. I was filming these geese and was getting some great shots. The first day, they were yellow and fluffy but, by the second day, they'd already turned a darker colour. Now, on the third day, I was eager to get some more photos.

Instead, I got a shock. There were no Canada geese on that pond, or anywhere around it. Two adults and five goslings, vanished into thin air.

I searched everywhere, and so did everyone else. We went up the stream that feeds into the pond, and into the woods, but those geese had gone.

I can tell you, I was cursing away, blaming the foxes or buzzards, or maybe a mink or a heron, for getting the little ones. Did something get the parents too, or did they fly away after their chicks got eaten?

Now, I know that's nature's way, that predators need prey to keep them alive, but I couldn't help being upset about those geese. The odd thing was, we couldn't find any sign of a struggle. Usually, when a fox or stoat or suchlike takes his prey, there's a sign of some kind of struggle – feathers lying about, or whatever. But there was nothing, not anywhere on the land, and we finally had to give up the search.

The next day, I was up early and out at the land, hoping for a miracle, that those geese would be there. But of course there was nothing but an empty nest.

It was a beautiful morning, warm and hazy, and full of birdsong. The bluebells were smelling like heaven and, finally, after a cold start to May, all the trees were at last in leaf. But all I could think about that morning was those geese. The pond looked empty without them, even though the dragonflies were out now. There were bulrushes and lilies on the pond. The heron wasn't there that morning. I wondered if he'd taken the goslings. Mind, I couldn't complain if he had. I wouldn't like it, but that's the way nature is. The grey heron is such a beautiful bird, and he's got to eat too. Still, I hoped he hadn't eaten those little goslings.

I remember the first grey heron that landed on my pond. I couldn't believe my eyes. The pond wasn't even finished, only half full, not yet stocked with fish. I was in my hide and looked out, and there he was. It was a gladsome sight, let me tell you. I was so pleased.

Still, the heron wasn't about that day so maybe he didn't get those chicks. I had a safari so I couldn't hang around. I left our land still puzzling over those Canadian geese. A few days later, I was at South Molton market again. I was talking to Penny Norman, my friend Bill Norman's daughter. She said to me, 'Johnny, I saw some Canadian geese down my way yesterday. Two adults and five little ones, down at the stream near our place.'

I couldn't believe it. They were the geese from our land, no question about it. They'd gone walkabout, following the stream below the pond down past Knowstone Mill, went up Crooked Oak to Higher Wadham, heading towards Pols Moor, towards Bill Norman's house. They were about a mile from their nest on our land.

I was excited as could be. As soon as market was over, Julie and I packed up the books and videos and photos, and I took off to where those geese were spotted, but there was no sign of them. I followed along the stream where they might have gone, and I searched all over the fields and woods. They'd disappeared again.

Later, I told everyone I knew about those geese, asking them to keep lookout for me. I felt better that they hadn't been eaten by a fox or stoat. But I was puzzling why they just upped and left. It was very unusual behaviour, and I hadn't seen anything like it before. That's one of the great things about wild animals and birds. You think you know their habits, but they can still do something out of the ordinary to keep you on your toes.

I heard a similar story about badgers. A farmer up on Dartmoor had two badger setts on his property, on opposite ends. He liked badgers, and he kept an eye out for them. This went on for several years until, one spring, he came out to look at the setts and one of them was empty. It was like looking at a ghost town, he said. The other sett was full of the newborn cubs but this one had been totally deserted. No sign of life at all, and no sign of any disturbance either. The badgers had upped and moved house, just like the geese.

I had a problem with badgers a few years back on our land. I'd built a wooden badger wheel to entice the animals on to our land, for I love badgers and hoped they would come stay at our place. That first year, no badgers appeared, none at all. I didn't know why; no one seemed to know. After talking to a badger expert, I found out. That year, we'd had a very dry April. Very unusual for Exmoor, it was. Now, badgers have their cubs in January, February and March, so by April they're getting weaned off their mother's milk and need food. Apparently, worms are the prime food for badger cubs. Would you believe, they need two hundred to three hundred worms a day! Because of that dry April, though, there were hardly any worms, so many cubs died off.

Luckily, the next year was better, and I got the badgers on our land at last. You never know what you're going to find when you start looking closely at the natural world.

But I was still worried about the Canada geese. Finally I heard that the parents and their goslings were found at George's place, Oak Tree Fisheries, but, sadly, only two of the goslings had survived.

CHAPTER 21

Cream Tea in My Hide

SPRINGTIME IS ALWAYS A BUSY TIME FOR US AT THE LAND, AND this year was even more hectic. I was filming this programme on birds for BBC4, and this was nesting time. I had fifteen cameras set up, trying to get photos of swallows, blackbirds, grey wagtails, wrens, rock pigeons. I was trying to film a peregrine too, and hoping for some barn owls. Woodpeckers, too. There were bird-boxes all over the place. I had a generator set up to run the computer in the cabin so I could see on the screen what was going on in those boxes. The swallows had eggs hatching, and I was trying to get my camera on to the wren's nest.

My days were filled to brimming. The good weather was sent from heaven, perfect for the things I wanted to do.

This was a typical day. I met the film crew at nine on the land, and we did some filming. I told the story of the Canadian geese on the film, and then about the woodpecker I was filming. I talked about the meadow grass and flowers that were enticing the butterflies on to our land. Then I went into the cabin with the film crew, and I talked about the boxes. After that, I checked the cameras again and looked at what I'd got on film. It was a busy morning.

At 1.30, I finally went home for dinner but, at 2.15, I was back in the village. There I saw two very nice people, Caroline and David, who live in Bishops Nympton. They gave me permission to film on their land, which was kind of them. There were some fox cubs there, and I wanted to get shots of them.

There were six cubs, right at the playful age, not very old. They'd made their den in the middle of a steep field. I hid myself in a hedge, stayed there all afternoon keeping an eye on that den, watching the cubs go in and out. They didn't go far, though. Not yet.

Finally, I went home, had my tea in a rush, gulping down some cold food to keep me going, and grabbed my still camera. I went right back to those fox cubs. I had on all my camouflage gear, plus mask and gloves, and settled down to take photos. I was lucky: I got some great footage. The best shot came at around nine that evening. I had been sitting there waiting while the vixen went off, hoping she'd come back with food for the cubs and I could film them eating. The cubs were all inside their den, waiting, like I was.

Then the vixen approached. She didn't have any food, but I got my best shots of fox cubs that night. Three of the cubs saw her coming and ran out to meet her, wanting a drink of milk. The wind must have been in the right direction, for those cubs came right near the hedge where I was hiding. I whipped off my gloves and started taking photos. They didn't notice me.

The vixen must have been tired, and maybe hungry too, for she tried to shake off those cubs as they grabbed on to her and started suckling her. But they were stubborn little sods and held on tight. She ran towards the den, and the cubs held on, their feet dangling right off the ground as the vixen tried to get away from them. She'd had enough. The fox cubs had had enough too; they were plump little things – well fed, for sure. But they were greedy for more. Those three were still holding on as the vixen went to the den, and then, would you believe, three more came out to suckle her.

That poor vixen had her work cut out for her. I thought about her as I finally made my way home. When her cubs slept and it was dark, she'd be out roaming, finding food for herself and her cubs.

I hoped she'd find a good supply of rabbits or mice, and not my Canadian geese, wherever they were.

I came home that night at 9.30, tired but happy. I've written in other books about how I learned to be patient and watchful stalking wild animals for food when I was a poacher in my young days. Those early days taught me the skills I needed for filming. It takes hours of waiting to take photos of wildlife. People ask me how I get my photos. 'I stay in one place,' I tell them.

My first shot of a kingfisher took five hours. I sat in a hide in an old armchair and stayed put, did nothing but wait. The same thing happened when I got a shot of a grey wagtail. I waited and watched and, when there was a patch of sunlight come out from behind a cloud, the bird finally spread its feathers out for me to photo. It was some sight, and worth the wait.

There's a story like that behind every photo I've taken.

Speaking of kingfishers, there's a lovely story about how the kingfisher came to be such a beautiful-coloured bird. Once upon a time or another, the kingfisher's feathers were all grey and colourless, not like the wonderful bright bird we see today. This was at the time that Noah built his ark. Noah eventually let the kingfisher off the ark, after weeks of waiting for the rains to stop. It had finally stopped, and the bird was told by Noah to go and find some dry land. The kingfisher was so happy to be free at last that it flew straight up to heaven! There, some of the blue of the sky rubbed off on him. He flew near the sun, and some of the sun's glow stained his chest. He was so happy, that kingfisher, flying about, free at last, above the water.

But then he suddenly remembered that Noah had asked him to find some dry land, which he finally did. But when he went back to tell Noah this, he couldn't find the ark. He searched and searched, but there was no sign of it anywhere. And to this day, this is why the kingfisher flies low over rivers: he's searching for Noah's ark.

Roxy told me today that we've got quite a few safaris booked in the next couple of months. Folk like to come out in spring to see the baby animals, to hear the cuckoo, spot birds nesting. September and October are busy too, when visitors come out to see the stag rutting. I start weeks ahead of time, going all over Exmoor keeping a close watch on the animals and the birds. I go to different places with each one, depending on where I've found bird nests and animal dens, where I've heard the cuckoo that year or seen where the Exmoor ponies are fond of gathering. Stuart goes along in another jeep when mine is full up. It's a busy time for me, with everything else going on, but I wouldn't have it any other way. With all the things I've got to do this time of year, I'm always grateful to all my family and friends who help out, either on the land or telling me about wild animals they've spotted, so I can track them down for the camera. It's the time of year too, though, when I miss old friends who have passed away, especially Tony Thorne.

I remember having Tony in my hide, not long before he died, about three years back now.

I had been lucky to have some lovely roe deer appear on our land, one a young stag, with his antlers just starting to grow. Tony wanted to see them, so I invited him and another old mate, Albert, into my hide for a cream tea and an evening of deer watching.

The hide on our land was finally finished, and I was using it a lot. I had armchairs in it and photos on the wall – even a pair of antlers! It was my home away from home, and I spent hours in there, so I wanted it nice.

Tony and Albert hadn't seen it since I'd decorated it all up. They thought it looked fantastic. Tony said, 'I think I'll have a holiday here, Johnny,' as he settled down in one of the armchairs.

Albert agreed it would be a fine place to spend a few weeks' holiday. They started talking about what they'd do. 'We could go boating on the pond, now couldn't we, Bertie?' said Tony.

'You don't know much about boats,' muttered Bertie.

'No, that's true, I don't know much about boats. But I could learn.'

They went on like this for a time. I said, 'Now, you two have to stop being so noisy. We're here to wait for the deer. No animal or bird will come near the hide if you're talking all the time.'

I believe I've mentioned before what a talker Tony was. Albert is too, especially when he was with Tony. The two of them grinned. Tony said, 'It's true we're noisy, Johnny. We'll just have to be quiet now, won't we? It's no good hiding and waiting for the deer if we keep on talking, isn't that right, Johnny? Bertie and I, we've got to stop talking.'

'Tony, will you please shut up?' I grabbed the plate of scones and jam and Devon cream. 'Here, have your tea, and mebbe that'll stop your gabbing for a bit.'

'Oh, Johnny, that looks wonderful! I guess we'll have to stop talking if we're going to eat all those.'

After we'd eaten those delicious scones that Julie had made for us, we got down to the business of waiting for wildlife. 'Wonderful tea,' Tony said, licking his lips. Tony lived alone and never married, so he appreciated Julie's home cooking more than anyone. Albert agreed, and they started talking about how good the strawberry jam tasted. They sounded like they'd settled into a long conversation about cream teas and suchlike.

I said, 'I've got to close the windows. You two are so noisy you'll scare every bird and animal for miles around.'

Tony laughed. He had a wonderful laugh, a kind of low, soft chuckle from deep in his throat. 'Well, Johnny, I think the more noise you make, the more you'll see. Don't you agree, Albert?'

Albert wasn't too sure about that. I said, 'Tony, I can see why you were never a good poacher. That's the craziest thing I ever heard of.'

I shut all the windows in the hide, and we settled down to see what would arrive. Tony and Albert kept up their chatter. They couldn't help it, that's just the way they were. Especially Tony, God bless him, wherever he is. He said now, 'Oh look, Johnny, there's a squirrel!'

'Luckily, squirrels don't mind noise,' grinned Albert.

'Oh, look at that lovely jay. Isn't he a beauty?'

'And there's a goldfinch on the bird feeder.'

I said, 'Now, look, you two, I'm going to open this

window so we can see the birds better. Just hush, all right, mates?'

I opened the window and Tony said, 'There now, we got a better view with that window open,' and all the birds flew away.

Finally it was evening, about eight o'clock, and starting to get dark. I said to the other two, 'Now's the time when the deer and the badgers should come out. We'll wait till a quarter to nine and then call it a day, all right? But you've got to be quiet. Not say a word, y'hear?'

Tony looked horrified. Albert said, 'Y'want us to stay quiet until a quarter to nine?' They both gaped at me as if I'd said something truly outrageous.

But they promised they'd try. And they did keep still long enough for a lovely roe deer to come out, and I got a chance to film it. But they didn't manage to stop talking for forty-five minutes – no chance.

When it was time to go, Tony said, 'I want to stay a bit longer. Can't we stay on a bit, Johnny?'

'No chance.'

'We do talk a bit, don't we?' Tony grinned at me.

'Oh, shut up, won't you?' I shook my head then grinned back at him. 'But it wouldn't be the same if you didn't rabbit on, Tony, now would it? It just wouldn't be the same.'

We had some right old times, did Tony and me and, wherever you are, mate, you'll be grinning away, thinking of our cream tea that day in the hide.

CHAPTER 22

Smugglers' Tales

WHEN I WAS A YOUNGSTER, I USED TO GO UP TO THE NORTH coast of Devon and Somerset with my mates now and again, to be by the sea. There are so many sandy bays to explore, and rocky inlets, and hidden combes which slope right down to the sea. Sometimes we'd find things, an old coin or some such. We never found anything valuable, but we liked to think whatever we did find had been left by one of the many smugglers that used to drop anchor in these secluded inlets.

Everyone knows about smuggling, how it was a way of life for hundreds of years on the coast of Exmoor. There are so many wild places on the moor where smugglers could hide their goods – caves and suchlike. They smuggled in tobacco and brandy, and also a lot of tea.

There must have been a certain satisfaction in drinking a nice cuppa, knowing you didn't have to pay a tax to the king on it. So many folk were in the smuggling business that it was a way of life, and many people thought nothing of it, even though it was illegal. A bit like poaching, I suppose. You did what you could to save a bit of money here and there and, as long as you didn't hurt anyone doing it, you didn't feel you were doing anything wrong.

But there are all sorts of stories of smuggling gone wrong. Like the boat captain from Brittany who didn't realize how far the tide went out at Weston-super-Mare. Not only was his boat stranded, but also all the kegs of brandy that he'd dumped overboard, expecting to pick up later. What a shock that must have been!

Then there were the smugglers at Minehead, who put out the story that, on dark nights, a phantom coach and horses pulling a hearse appears from the sea and drives along the shore. Anyone who sets eyes on it would die within the year, so their tale went. Of course, even those who didn't quite believe in the superstition didn't want to risk it, just in case, so the smugglers had the freedom of the beach, with no prying eyes to stop them. Cunning, those sods were!

Purbeck Bay in Dorset was known to have many smugglers in the old days. There was one such chap who had the misfortune to be living right next door to the customs officer of the village. This smuggler had a horse, a very well-trained horse who helped his master in his undercover activities. The horse used to stand at the harbour to receive the illegal goods which were loaded on to his back. He was so well trained that the smuggler didn't even have to go down to the harbour, but just wait at home. The horse would come plodding back with the smuggled items, and the smuggler unloaded them and hid them away until they could be sold.

One night, that poor horse must have been tired, or had a bad day or some such. Instead of stopping at the smuggler's house, he stopped next door, at the custom man's house. The officer heard the *clomp clomp clomp* of the horse's hooves, and came out. Imagine his surprise and delight when he saw all that stolen booty right in front of him!

In another place in Dorset, Durstone Bay, the tubs of smuggled goods were sunk into the harbour for a time. The trouble was, the sand was soft silt and the barrels sank. So the smugglers put them on wooden planks so that they'd stay up a bit from the silty bottom. To mark where the kegs were, they tied a rope from the tubs to a bottle with a cork that floated on the water.

This worked very well until, one day, the lady of the town came down to the harbour for some reason or another. She must have been a bit bored because she started asking the fishermen about all those bottles with corks in them floating in the harbour. 'Well, now, them be lobster pots, ma'am,' they told her.

So would you believe, this lady now decided she wanted to see how lobsters were caught. She asked the men to pull up the rope so she could see the lobster pots for herself. The men wanted to refuse, but they couldn't, because she was a lady married to one of the great lords and, in those days, they made the rules in that place.

Imagine her surprise when up came the smuggled brandy, or whatever it was they were bringing in that time. Unluckily for the smugglers, the local customs officer was at the harbour, and the game was up.

But no doubt the smugglers found a way to get around this difficulty. There are so many stories about how the more famous ones outwitted the law.

Roger Ridout was one such man. He was born in 1736 and was a famous smuggler on the Dorset coast. Once, he had to escape from his house using a sheet tied into a rope to get out of the high bedroom window, when the officers of the law were banging on the front door. Another time, he was met by an armed customs man who asked him what he was carrying. As luck would have it, he happened to be carrying a bottle of some kind of strong balm on him, along with some smuggled brandy. Roger Ridout said to the customs man, 'Would'ee like to 'ave a smell, sir?' The officer, thinking it was the brandy, had a big whiff and got a faceful of balm. It was so over-powering that he stepped back, dropped his gun, and the smuggler was able to push him in a ditch and run away, free once more.

This Roger, he had a horse name Ridout's Ratted Tail.

You can guess from the name what kind of a tail that horse had! Roger had special words he'd whisper into the horse's ear on certain occasions, usually when he was in trouble. On one occasion, the smuggler was surrounded by a group of nasty rivals who were determined to get rid of Roger, for he was a far better smuggler. As they tried to pull him from his horse, he whispered in the creature's ear, 'What did'ee do fer thy king?'

Now, I don't know why he used those particular words, but they always had a magic effect on that horse. It began rearing and bucking so ferociously that it knocked the door clear off a nearby house. Roger held on, the others ran like hell and, once again, the smuggler got away free.

The big place for smuggling in those old days, though, was down in Cornwall. All those bays and inlets and harbours, many hidden by cliffs and tucked away in odd little places, were perfect. It was a great way to make a bob or two and, as I've said before, for many people it was a way of life.

There were plenty of customs officers and coastguard men who tried to stop the smugglers, but sometimes it was a losing battle. Luckily, they often had a sense of humour, as did this one officer who found a keg washed up on the sand. He called together twelve men from the town, all good, honest folk, and told them about the barrel. Then he proclaimed that those men were going to be the jury that had to judge the contents of the barrel. They would be the official tasters for the Crown. If they decided the cask contained spirits, it would be confiscated for the Crown. But if they then decided the brandy tasted of salt, that the sea water had got into it, then the cask would be smashed and the contents would soak into the sand.

Then he did a funny thing. He gave the men a friendly nod and told them to meet him at the barrel as soon as they'd gone home and got a bucket or jug or suchlike. By and by, they all got together at that cask. All the men had a good long drink and decided it was certainly brandy. Solemnly, the officer told them they now had another duty to the Crown. They had to take another long swig to see if it tasted of sea water.

Each man did. And everyone made terrible faces and rolled their eyes, as if they'd just had a long drink of the most horrible brew ever tasted. Some even clutched their stomachs in agony. Finally, the officer asked them if they agreed that the brandy was tainted with sea water. 'Oh yes,' they all cried out. 'Oh yes, terrible stuff, no good to the Crown at all.'

So of course the officer had no choice but to smash the barrel and let the contents spill out over the sandy beach. But you can be sure there were many jugs and buckets and whatnot on hand so that not all that good brandy ended up back in the sea. And you can be sure that the customs official had the biggest bucket of them all.

*

The Lizard, in Cornwall, was another place full of smugglers. There is a well-known place called Prussia Cove which was famous for that. Many men got rich around there through smuggling, even the MP for Grampound, a Mr Philip Hawkins. When he died, he left £600 to the king. It was his conscience money. That was getting on for three hundred years ago, so you can imagine how much that would be worth now.

Talking about a lot of money, there was a smuggler called Enoch who came into possession of five hundred one-pound notes. The trouble was, the bank that had issued those banknotes had gone bust. His money wasn't worth a thing. What was worse was that it wasn't just his money, but belonged to his family. They would all be penniless!

So this Enoch called a meeting of the whole family. He had the idea of going to Brittany to use the notes to buy some good brandy. It would take everyone in the family to make the scheme work, though, for it had to be done quickly, before the French knew that the bank had gone bust. Everyone would have to keep it a tight secret too, which would be difficult with so many people in his large family involved.

Well, you know, Enoch's cunning plan worked. Not one member of that family let on what was up. They managed to get hold of boats and sneak over to the coast of France, buy the illegal goods and get them on board, and then get back without anyone in Cornwall knowing what they were up to. They worked so fast that they got that brandy back home before the French got whiff of anything wrong. Everything had worked perfectly and, let me tell you, when it was all over, they were the happiest family in Cornwall.

There must be dozens more stories about that time, and who knows how many of them are true? Some must be, for the tales told are still around even now, a couple of hundred years later. And no doubt they'll still be told in another couple of hundred years.

CHAPTER 23

Snow and Strife

THIS TIME OF YEAR, IT SEEMS LIKE EVERYONE AND EVERYTHING IN the West Country is busy getting on with things, the birds with their nesting and laying eggs and hatching their chicks, the animals with their young ones. Farmers are out and about starting to cut silage, preparing the ground for sowing. And so many people are involved with the tourist industry now, so shops and cafés that have been shut all winter are opening. Everywhere, new B&Bs and guesthouses are springing up. There is a good kind of excitement, this time of year, when everything is growing and coming alive after the hard winters. Some of our towns and villages seem quiet and empty in January and February. There are a lot of people who own second homes on Exmoor, and it can empty a place. But now they are starting to come back and open their houses, with the weather so warm and perfect this spring.

Winters, on the other hand, are wet on Exmoor, wet and cold. This year was particularly icy, and we had a fair bit of snow. The little lanes and country roads were shut off for days. Farming on the moor is tough in winter, with frozen pipes, power cuts, days when the milk lorry can't get in and the dairy farmers' milk goes to waste. In my young days, it was worse. A snowfall could cut you off for weeks.

I was only a year old during the famous freeze of 1940 which gripped all of England and the rest of Europe as well. The temperature plummeted down well below freezing and stayed there for ages. Exmoor was covered in ice and frost and snow. In Exford, a car was able to drive over the frozen river, it was that bad. It must have been a hell of a time for the locals. The drifts on the moor were six to eight feet high. As kids, we used to hear stories about how people could walk right over the hedgerows, the drifts were so high.

One of the men talked about for years afterwards was a postman at Simonsbath called Frank Vigers. It was said he delivered the post every day, crawling over frozen snowdrifts on his hands and knees. It took five and a half hours to deliver mail seven miles away.

That year, there was also something they called rain-freeze. Rain turned to ice as it came down, and covered everything – trees, plants, telegraph wires. It didn't get above freezing temperature for days, and many plants and shrubs died because of that frozen rain.

The blizzards of 1962–3 are the ones I remember. The snow started at the end of December and came down with a howling wind. All the little lanes on the moor, and near it, leading to all the villages, were soon cut off. Before anyone had a chance to recover, a second lot came at the beginning of January. Farms and houses and whole villages were cut off for weeks. Helicopters were used to deliver food and medicine. It was especially tough for the old folk, and those who were ill. But the kids loved it. There was a lot of sledging and ice skating.

Dartmoor has had some nasty blizzards at times too. I know a farmer there who had a hard time in the snow-storm of 1976. That year, too, the drifts were so bad that it took days to shovel out the vet's car, which he'd abandoned when it started to snow. They had a hard time finding it; they knew it was under there somewhere. This was outside this farmer's place – Danny is his name, and he still farms in the West Country. He had four or five kids at the time I tell of, all little. His electricity had gone, but he had big open fires and plenty of wood. The family moved into the sitting room, all huddled together for warmth, where they stayed day and night, along with a couple of piglets. The sow had given birth a day or so back, and these two were the runts, not doing so well in the freezing cold. The littlest children treated those piglets like toys, dressing them up in dolls' clothes and trying to play with them. They didn't like it much, squealed their bloody heads off, driving Lizzie, the farmer's wife, crazy.

She was the one stuck with them. The farmer was out trying to feed his pigs and dig his sheep out of the snow-drifts. There was no feed for the animals until a helicopter came along and dropped some hay down. Another helicopter had to come for one of the neighbour's wives, who was having a baby. Lizzie had to have her two kids too, while all this was going on, and food was short. But she had a bloody great sack of potatoes, and another of onions, so she made that do. Potato and onion pie, potato and onion soup, mashed potatoes with fried onions on top – the family lived on that for days, until finally the drifts melted a bit and Danny could get the tractor out and go to the shops.

The way Lizzie stood all this was a wonder to all, for she wasn't a West Country maid. She was a city girl, born and bred in London and New York and goodness knows what other cities. She met Danny at a sheep show when visiting a friend in Exeter. Lizzie had never even seen a sheep before, hard as it is to believe, and she'd seen some advert for this agricultural show somewhere or other and thought it would be a right laugh. There was to be a sheep-shearing competition, and Danny had entered, reckoning that he could shear a sheep as fast as any man.

It was up somewhere in the middle of Dartmoor. Now, remember this was in the 1960s, when the moor was wilder and more isolated than it is now. It was mostly locals, the ones born here, who lived in the villages and farms; not like now, when there are often more visitors and second-homers than locals. So Lizzie – though she called herself Elizabeth then – thought she was on another planet, having just come from the big city.

It was a fine day, that day of the sheep shearing. Lizzie was taking photos like nobody's business, wanting to show them to her city friends. She took one of Danny as he was getting the trophy for winning the competition, looking all sweaty but big and strong, and grinning like crazy. In those days, you took the film and got it developed, which is what Lizzie did when she got to London. That's where she was living at the time. She liked the look of Danny – maybe it was that crazy grin, or maybe those broad shoulders. Whatever it was, it caused Lizzie to track him down. She went back to Exeter to stay with her friend. The two of them went back to the village where the shearing took place, asked around. Danny was living with his mum and dad, small farmers with a bit of land, a few sheep. Lizzie found him, gave him the photo she took.

It wasn't long before they were married and living on their own place up on Dartmoor. The trouble started the first night they got back from their honeymoon. They couldn't afford to go far, so they spent a week in a tent up on the coast, near Porlock. It rained all week, so Danny told about it later. That didn't please Lizzie, her having a romantic idea about country life. Danny hadn't told her about the rain and the mud and those harsh winters on the moor.

When they got back, one of the sows was farrowing. A mate of Danny's had been looking after the farm while they were away, but he'd gone. Now, this sow was a devil of a pig. She'd savaged all her first litter, and Danny was afraid she'd do it to her second, so he was determined to keep an eye on her. The trouble was, he had a ewe giving birth down the bottom of his field, and she was having trouble. The lamb was feet first, and Danny was needed to pull it out.

So he did the only thing he could. He told Lizzie to get into the pig pen and keep an eye on that sow. 'Just sit on that wooden fence between pens, out of her way. She's fierce.' He put a plank of wood in Lizzie's hand. 'When she pops one out, get in there, grab the piglet and toss it gently over into the other pen. But keep your eye on that sow. She'll savage you if she can't get to her newborn.'

'Is that what this stick is for?' Lizzie couldn't believe what Danny was telling her to do.

'Yup. Just whack her one if she comes near you.'

That was Lizzie's first night in her new home, perched in the pig pen with a savage sow. The neighbours all made bets that she'd be gone before a month was out, but she and Danny are still there, getting on now, all the kiddies grown. The neighbours had a right old laugh, though, while Lizzie was getting used to country ways. She was such a city girl, wearing short skirts with her wellie boots, her knees all covered with mud, the bangles on her wrists and rings in her ears getting all tangled with straw. The postman once found her in tears in the kitchen of the farmhouse. She was sitting on the floor with her head in her hands and a bunch of dead pigeons around her. She'd reached up to get something out of a top shelf and the birds had all dropped down on her, right on her head, like it was raining bloody pigeons. Danny had gone out shooting for grub, like we all did in those days, and bagged enough for more than one pigeon pie. Lizzie was out when he came in, so he tossed the birds up in the top cupboard then went out to check his sheep.

The funny thing was, the postman told everyone later at the pub, she wouldn't talk to Danny for days. No one could understand why she got so upset over a few pigeons. Poor Danny, he had to pluck and eat the birds himself. Lizzie didn't want anything to do with them. She said she couldn't imagine eating pigeons anyway, that they were filthy things that mucked up buildings and everything else with their nasty ways. Danny said there were country pigeons and city pigeons, two different things altogether, but Lizzie said any dead pigeon that fell on her head when she was minding her own business was a nasty one.

Lizzie was all right, though. She learned how to live up on Dartmoor, plunging right into life on the farm. There were a few setbacks, mind. Like the day Danny and his mate, who was helping out on the place, killed a couple of chickens for Lizzie to cook for dinner one day. They decided to have a laugh and, after they'd wrung the chickens' necks, they threw the bodies into the kitchen, where Lizzie was trying to figure out how to bake scones. Now, anyone who's had to kill a chicken knows that, even after their necks have been chopped off, they jig about for a few seconds. So there were these two headless chickens jumping about in Lizzie's kitchen.

Lizzie screamed the place down. She didn't think it was a bit funny, and neither did Danny after she'd given him a piece of her mind. I believe it was the last joke he played on Lizzie and, after that, their marriage got a bit smoother.

CHAPTER 24

Having Less and Making Do

THERE ARE MORE VISITORS THAN EVER NOW IN THE WEST Country. Some decide to stay, and make a place for themselves here. Sometimes, I'm amazed at how different life is in these parts now. Yet I still meet old-timers, some twenty years older than me, leading the lives they've always lived.

There's an old man, Ben, of more than ninety years old, living on a bit of land he bought as a lad, up on Bodmin Moor, about seventy years ago. He meant to put a house up there one day but in the end he never bothered, or never got permission, or whatever. He didn't give up his land, though. No, he hung on to it, living in the rough, in a makeshift tent on his land. Nobody told him not to, so he bought an old caravan, kept it there and lived in that for a few years. Finally, he grew some vegetables to sell at market. The planning authorities said he could build a shed to store them in, so that's what he did. What they didn't say was that he could live there too. But he does. They've given up trying to get him out. He doesn't shoot game any more, as his eyes aren't too good, but he's got a pension and buys cheap meat at the local butcher, cooks it on a camp stove, makes a big stew of it with edible plants he's gathered here and there. He doesn't have much, just a bed and a chair and that camp stove, but he's got one hell of a lot of books. They are lined all along the walls of his shed, and in piles on the floor. I'm sure it helps with the insulation. That shed must be sodding cold in winter. But old Ben, he's got a couple of Calor gas heaters and puts on a couple more jumpers. Come winter, he's well prepared, especially as he still makes his own wine and stocks up for the cold months.

There are others like Ben up on all the moors, and in other isolated spots, places still a bit cut off from the rest of the world. Not many, though. They're dying out. When they go, their tumbledown houses and sheds will be all prettied up, and maybe go for second homes. Maybe that's why folks tell of these things, why they are talked about. Everyone knows these old-timers won't be around much longer, and there aren't many people like that any more to take their place.

Some of those people like Ben have wonderful stories to tell. Ben tells of his sister, gone now, like all his brothers. She was called Agnes and was the only girl amongst six children. She was the youngest too. At first she was spoiled rotten, being the girl, but when the mother died young, Agnes had to do all the cooking and cleaning for her father and five older brothers while they went out to work on the farm. She was only fourteen. It was hard work for a woman in those days, all that washing by hand, cooking on an ancient wood-burning stove. They didn't have much money, so it was tough. Agnes had to do all the kitchen and housework, and help out on the farm as well. Her hands were rough and red from all that washing and peeling, and she was plagued with backache even when young. By the time she was twenty, she walked with a stoop in her shoulders, she was that worn.

It sounded harsh, Ben said, when he told people about his sister, but that's the way things were in those days. All the brothers worked hard too, from dawn to dusk, but Agnes, being a woman, had to do things like get up before dark and get the fire going in the stove for breakfast, heat water, and suchlike.

Ben said he and his brothers thought their sister was an angel. He said she had the most beautiful hair he'd ever seen on a woman. It was a pale kind of ashy blond, silk-like. All the brothers admired it. It was so beautiful that they didn't let her cut it, and took turns brushing it at night. They brought her little gifts too. Wildflowers from the meadow, for Agnes loved flowers. They picked whortleberries for her and, sometimes, when they had a bit of spare cash, some special treat from the market, like fresh strawberries, or a small bunch of heather they bought for a few pence from one of the gypsy women who used to come around selling it, for luck and good fortune.

It wasn't long before the village lads all over Dartmoor started flocking about, wanting to court Agnes. Ben and his brothers wouldn't hear of it, though. They thought their sister far too good for any of the local blokes. In fact, they thought their sister too good for any man, and kept them well away.

So Agnes kept on keeping house for her five brothers, even after their father died. They still wouldn't let her cut her hair, even though it was streaked with grey by then. It came down past her waist, Ben said, but she put it all up on top of her head during the day.

Then she had her fortieth birthday, and everyone knew for sure she would live and die an old maid, as they called unmarried women in those days. But Agnes surprised everyone. She ran off with a man up from Cornwall. She'd met him at a sheep sale at Hatherleigh Market, but she kept her meeting secret. She knew her brothers would chase him off, like they'd chased the others over the years.

So, one night, Agnes sneaked out the kitchen door, taking nothing but a few clothes in a cardboard box. This man was waiting at the crossroads, and off they went, down to Cornwall somewhere, where he had a small-holding. She left a short note saying she was eloping, but not who she was eloping with.

Ben and his brothers found out soon enough. Cornwall was a long way away in those days, no motorways or dual carriageways, only windy lanes, so it was a few days before they found their sister. They were going to bring her home, by force if necessary, but in the end they let her be.

At this point in Ben's story, people usually said, 'Oh, you must have seen how happy she was, having her own home.' But he always put them right. 'Happy? Don't know about that. He was a Cornishman, how could anyone be happy with 'ee? No, we let her be because she'd bluddy well cut all her hair off. Can you believe it? Right off to her shoulders! Me and my brothers were that upset we came right on home. Didn't see Agnes again for years.'

When Agnes left, none of the brothers had the heart for farming any more, so they sold up, split the profits. That's when Ben bought his bit of land where he lives now. Two brothers went off to Australia to work on farms, one went off with the travellers after meeting a gypsy woman in the pub, and one became a tramp, sleeping out in the woods and roaming both Dartmoor and Exmoor until he died at the age of eighty.

'Agnes got her share of the farm too,' Ben said when he told this story. 'Good thing too, because that Cornishman she married was sodding useless. Managed to bankrupt his smallholding by gambling and drinking and then ran off with another woman. He tried to get Agnes back when she got her share of the money, but by then she didn't want him. She bought the place herself and stayed there happily on her own until the day she died. She never did a lick of cooking after he left either. Lived off cold meats and tinned beans which she didn't even heat up. She'd had enough of cooking, thank you very much, she'd say, and vowed she'd never cook another damn thing as long as she lived. Trouble was, she felt the same about housework. Refused to do much in the house, so it got to be a right smelly mess. But Agnes didn't care. For the first time in her life, she said, she was living life the way she wanted.'

Ben stopped at this point in his story and shrugged his shoulders before going on. 'Can't say as I blame her. She was contented, like, y'know? Still is, far as I know. Leastways, she was a few months back, when she took three buses all the way out from Cornwall, to come out and see me.'

In many ways we were lucky, in those old days. Though we didn't have much, we lived more or less how we wanted. If we couldn't afford to buy meat or fish, we poached it from the rivers and from the land. We felt it belonged to everyone, the land, not just a few people.

In the villages and countryside, people did all sorts of things to make ends meet. I've told in my first book how I used to catch and skin moles as well as stoats, foxes, weasels. I used to get two bob for a stoat or weasel skin and five shillings for a fox. It was a way to earn money for a young lad. My parents couldn't afford to give me any- thing. They fed me and cared for me and were wonderful parents, but I had to help by earning a bob or two myself.

Everyone I knew lived like this. People with a bit of land, maybe an acre or two, kept chickens, geese, maybe a pig or two for their own use. Danny, the farmer up on Dartmoor, told me about a neighbour of his who bought a hundred newborn chicks on a whim. He was at Hatherleigh market, and this man came in with all these day-old chicks for sale. He wanted to get rid of them, and offered a good price to anyone who would take the whole lot. This farmer – he was called Norman, I believe – had to think quick. He was in there selling a couple of old ewes, and they didn't fetch a good price. He had a wife and a load of kids – six or seven, if I remember rightly – who were getting older and hungrier.

Norman took the lot. He figured he was on to a good deal. He knew all about raising day-old chicks, as he'd done it before. He knew damn well that at least half would die before they reached the eating stage. If he was lucky, he'd have fifty left. Ten he'd keep to feed the family on, sticking them in his old freezer, and the other forty he'd pluck and sell at market.

Well, you wouldn't believe it, but only two out of a hundred of those day-old chicks died. Norman couldn't believe it. Every day he'd go out into the chicken shed, and every day there would be ninety-eight growing chickens cluck clucking around his feet. He fenced off a bit of grass for a chicken run when they outgrew the shed, and soon had to enlarge it as they grew and grew. It drove him crazy, going out there every day with all the slops and leftovers from dinner to feed the chickens, wondering why they weren't dying off like they were supposed to. Soon he was going about all the neighbours asking them to save him the leftover food they were going to bin so that he could boil it up for his chickens. He was spending a bloody fortune on chicken food.

It wasn't long before those chickens were ready to be eaten. Instead of killing and plucking the fifty birds he'd expected, he had ninety-eight to do. His wife was busy having another baby, so she wasn't any help. So he had to do it all himself, as well as all the other work around the farm.

Meanwhile, those chickens were growing bigger and bigger. He could only do so many in a week, and they were growing every day. He'd go into market with the chickens he'd plucked, and each week they'd be bigger and bigger. Finally, they got to be the size of a small turkey.

In the end, he gave up. He brought the last twenty chickens – huge, they were, about 15lbs each – into market, packed into two large wooden crates. They were alive, and making an almighty row with their clucking and cawing. He didn't get much for them, but he didn't care. He was rid of them at last. Like he said to everyone in the market who would listen, 'There's only a limited number of chickens a man can pluck, and that's the truth.'

Norman wasn't the only one fed up with chickens. For weeks, his kids were trading the chicken legs and wings they brought for their packed lunches for anything else –

pasties, cheese sandwiches, fish paste, anything. To this day, I've heard tell that none of them will touch the meat, and they'll all be well over sixty by now.

Like I said, people did all sorts of things to make a bit of spare cash in those days. All us lads used to do odd jobs on the farms around the village. They weren't big farms like many of them are now. Most farmers struggled along, like the two women who had twenty acres or so over near the Devon/Somerset border. Now, they must have been seventy-five if they were a day, and they still made their living from this farm. They kept about fifty ewes and a half-dozen cows. When the cows were in heat, they'd borrow the bull belonging to the neighbour up the road to come service the animals. This bull was a big red South Devon bull, a ton and a half of weight. The neighbour used to open the gate of his field and walk that bull up the public road whenever he was needed. After he did his job, the neighbour came back and walked his bull home. Luckily, there weren't as many cars on the road in those days, because that bull took his time. You couldn't rush him.

Anyway, these farming ladies had hens too, and they sold their eggs up on the side of the road. There was an honesty box for the cash, and I never heard of anyone cheating those two women, or anyone else for that matter. Not in those honesty boxes, no way. Nowadays, I hear that people have to put locks on them or all the money would get nicked. I've even heard of entire cash boxes being lifted, along with all the eggs or plants or whatever products were being sold.

Now that saddens me. I'm not saying that people were saints in those days, not a bit of it, but folk did respect the honesty box. I've heard it said that times are bad now, people out of jobs, and that's why people steal the cash out of roadside boxes, but times were worse then. Money was a lot harder to come by. And we might have poached and nicked cider from local shops now and again, but one thing we never did was take the cash from those boxes.

Anyway, like I was saying, these two women – Miss Moore and Miss Roberts, they were called – ran this farm on their own. When they needed a hand with something they called on a lad called Pete who lived in the nearby village. Now, this Pete was about seventeen or eighteen at the time, and he needed the money so that he could go out to the pub on a Saturday night. He liked his cider, did Pete, just like the rest of us. He didn't have a regular job, but worked here and there when he could. He didn't much like working for the two lady farmers, because they didn't pay much, and they were always late in paying him. Never had it to hand, if you know what I mean. So poor Pete, he had to go back several times before he got that cash in his hand.

Miss Moore and Miss Roberts used to call on him when it was time to clean out the calf shed. Those two used to buy in calves now and again and sell them off when they were worth a bit more. Like many of the farmers around, they made do with whatever sheds were on the property.

This shed was like many of those old sheds, made of stone or concrete and wood with a tin roof. They had one thing in common, and that was a little narrow door. That door made it impossible for a tractor with a front-end loader to get in, so the shed had to be cleaned by hand. Miss Moore and Miss Roberts used to wait as long as they could before they called in Pete to clean it. They'd just pile more straw on top of the dung and shit until the calves' backs were practically touching the roof of the shed.

Pete hated that job. He had to shift all that stuff with nothing but an ancient dung fork. It took him two days. The worst of it was, one of those farmer ladies was usually stood right there next to him as he worked, giving advice now and again. Stuff like, 'Don't forget that corner over there,' or, 'Be careful how much dung you put on that fork, boy.' Like Pete said, it's only shovelling shit, not something you need a diploma in.

Pete had to take the dung forkful by forkful over to a dung spreader sat at the edge of their field. It belonged to a neighbouring farmer, who would come along with his tractor and spread the stuff on the field. The dung spreader was across the yard, and Pete had to carry the stuff over there and throw it in.

Those two ladies had an old sheep dog, about fifteen or sixteen years old, blind in one eye and stiff as a post with the rheumatism. He didn't do much but lie in the sun all day. Trouble was, his spot in the sun one day was right under Pete's feet. He tripped right over that damn dog and, as he did, the shit flew from the fork, through the air and landed right on Miss Moore's head.

'I couldn't have done it better if I'd stopped to take aim,' Pete told everyone at the pub later.

Miss Moore screamed as if she'd been hit with a bullet. Miss Roberts came running out and started shrieking as well when she saw her. Now, Miss Moore was tall and skinny and Miss Roberts was short and round. Pete said it was the funniest thing he'd ever seen, little Miss Roberts jumping up and down like a crazy hare trying to knock off the cow shit and straw running off Miss Moore's long, thin back and shoulders and arms. The two of them were yelping and squealing like little pigs. The sheep dog added his barking to the din. Pete just stood there, not knowing what in the hell to do.

Then, you know, he did a terrible thing. He admitted later it was a terrible thing, but he just couldn't help it. He started to laugh. He laughed so hard that he had to sit down right in the middle of the yard and hide his face in his hands. The funny thing was, the two lady farmers thought he was crying, and upset and hysterical over what he'd done. So after Miss Moore had more or less cleaned herself off, they bundled Pete into the house and gave him a stiff drink of brandy to revive him. Then Miss Moore decided she needed one too, and so did Miss Roberts, and before long the three of them were all laughing and merry as can be.

CHAPTER 25

Roaring Stags and a Coach of Bones

I WAS OVER TO DULVERTON A FEW DAYS AGO, AND UP NEAR Barle Valley. I stopped to watch a couple of deer grazing, two young hinds. It was a beautiful day, the sun making shadows through the new green of the trees. I stayed and watched for a bit, enjoying the peace and quiet.

It's not so quiet here in autumntime. There's an annual competition up at Draydon Rails, which looks out over Barle Valley. It's a roaring competition – some folk call it bolving, but I've always called it roaring – and you've never heard such sounds in your life if you've never been to Exmoor in the autumn.

Roaring is what the red stags do during the rutting season. It's their mating call, and it's one hell of a sound, like an almighty roar coming right from the belly of the animal up to the ends of his great antlers. It's an amazing sound, wonderful if you're not in the way of a huge, jealous, galloping stag full of fury answering that call and raring for a fight with his rival.

But on a certain day in October, it isn't only the rutting stags that make that sound. Exmoor has its annual roaring competition. There are at least a dozen men entering, from all over, not just hereabouts. They all take turns bellowing out the rutting cries, and they get points if a stag down in the valley answers them. I tell you, those stags can get jealous of their hinds, and if they hear the roar of another stag, they can be wild. A man can be roaring away and have a stag come charging right up to the fence he's at. It can be bloody scary, believe me. I've seen stags fighting during rutting season, and I know how fierce they are.

Some of the people who enter the competition have been practising since they were kids, growing up somewhere in the countryside or visiting it often, watching the deer closely, listening to the sounds of the stags.

The competition is growing bigger every year – hundreds of people come to watch – and I had the honour of being one of the judges one year. It was a great evening, a good laugh, and after everyone had done their roaring we all piled back to Dulverton, to the Rock House Inn. A lot of cider was drunk, amongst other things. There was an auction too, with the proceeds going to the Devon Air Ambulance. The place was heaving, but luckily no one tried their vocal cords on roaring again. It was all very well outside in the valley, but it would've deafened us all inside that pub.

Dulverton is one of my favourite towns on Exmoor. It's got a lot going for it, and not just the roaring competition! There are some nice shops and great pubs, and an old church that still has the thirteenth-century tower on it, although the rest of the medieval building is gone. In the churchyard, though, there's the stump of what's called the Belfry Tree. It's all that remains of a huge sycamore tree that was very old. Leaning against the ancient tower are two iron belts that were once used successfully to hold the split trunk of the tree together. It's supposed to be the first recorded example of tree surgery.

I think that just about every church in the West Country has some kind of story attached to it. Some true, like the ancient sycamore tree and the way it was held together, and others obviously legends. One of my favourite stories of how a church was built is about Brentor church on Dartmoor. It goes like this.

Many, many years ago, there was a very rich man, a merchant, who got caught in a terrible storm at sea. It lasted the whole fearsome night, and everyone on the boat thought for sure they were going to drown. So the merchant prayed, 'Lord, if you save my life, I'll build a church on the highest point on land I can see.'

Well, the good Lord saved his life and, sure enough, because this was somewhere off the coast of Plymouth, when the merchant was washed up on shore the next day, waterlogged but not drowned, he looked out over the horizon, and there was the highest point, Brentor. True to his word, he built his church there, and it's one of the prettiest in Dartmoor, a tiny stone chapel perched right on top of the rocky hill.

Of course, being Dartmoor, there's another story, if this one is too ordinary for you! Like on Exmoor, the devil has been known to lurk around Dartmoor, making mischief. Some of the old stories tell that old Lucifer was involved in the building of the Brentor church. What happened was this. The devil was so mad that the merchant had been saved that he went into an almighty sulk. He went to Brentor, where the church was being built, and every night, when the workmen had gone home, he knocked down everything that had been done that day.

Next day and night, the same thing happened. This was getting bloody discouraging, as you can imagine. The merchant didn't know what to do, so he sat down and said another little prayer. This was to his favourite saint, St Michael. Now don't ask me why this was his favourite saint, because I don't know. He was probably many people's favourite saint, for there are many churches named for him. Whatever the reason, this merchant asked St Michael to help him get rid of the devil so that he could finish the church, to keep his promise to the Lord.

You know, St Michael must have been an easygoing soul, for he sat up all that night waiting for the devil to appear. When he did, St Michael dropped a huge piece of Dartmoor granite on the devil's heel, and off he went, limping and feeling right sorry for himself. He never came back again, and the church was finally built. It's called St Michael's and now you know why. Oh, the bit I like about this story is that folk say that's why the church is so small. The merchant couldn't afford the huge grand church he'd planned on building, as it cost so much to keep rebuilding it after the devil knocked it down.

Telling that story reminds me of going to Okehampton last year, to give a talk at the school there. Right on the edge of the town is a castle, built in the eleventh century, up on a hill. That is, it's the ruin of a castle, because it was demolished by Henry VIII's men. There was an ancient deer park surrounding the castle, and that was destroyed too. You can still walk in the woods of some of the old park, and it's a beautiful place. In the spring, the grass under the mossy trees is filled with primroses then wood anemones and bluebells. There are some very old trees there, some wonderful oak and ash. In the autumn, the leaves on the beech trees glow with colour.

The castle looms above the park, quite impressive even now, but it must have been a sight to see before the king set his men on it. There's another sight to see around the castle too, if the locals can be believed. They say that the skeleton ghost of Lady Mary Howard haunts the lanes around there, riding in her coach pulled by skeleton horses.

It seems this Lady Mary was not a very nice woman. She married four times and outlived all her husbands. The story is, she murdered them all, but who knows if this is true or not.

She must have done something pretty nasty, though, for she is condemned to travel throughout eternity from Tavistock to Okehampton Castle, the distance being round about 16-odd miles. The castle was part of the Fitzford estates in Tavistock, which was Lady Mary Howard's home.

Every night, a fearsome sight appears outside Fitzford House. A huge, ugly, black dog with burning red eyes comes out of the gate. If you happen to see this dog, you'd better watch out, for the ghost of Lady Mary will be following it. She comes in a coach made of bones and skulls which rattle as her headless coachman drives her along. Lady Mary is dressed all in spooky white, and sits there, deadly silent, while the black dog leads the coach to Okehampton Castle.

Now this castle is set on a grassy mound and, every night, Lady Mary Howard has to pick a blade of grass and take it back with her to Fitzford House. She puts each bit of grass on a stone there and then disappears with her dog and coach until the next night.

Because of her wickedness, she has to do this every single night, until every blade of grass is gone from the mound of Okehampton Castle. And as it's a damn great hillock, I can't see her finishing her task for a long time to come.

That's the legend of Lady Mary Howard, as I've been told, but I've also heard tell that that poor woman has been much maligned. The truth seems to be that it was her father who was the wicked one. He got very rich when he was only a young man, about twenty-one or so, and started sowing his wild oats around Tavistock. Now, many young men about are wild, as I know very well from my own young days, but this man, John, went from wildness to wickedness. He had a terrible temper and lashed out at everyone – friends, family and servants – until, finally, two men were murdered right on the doorstep of his house, Fitzford House. No one ever found out who committed the murder, but it was common knowledge that John had something to do with it.

Poor Mary was hated by everyone because of her father, even though he committed suicide at the age of thirty-one. She was only nine years old at the time and was sold by the King of England, James I, to some earl up north, who married her off at the age of twelve to one of his brothers.

So you see, she had a sad old life. She had only one marriage to a man she loved, and he died of natural causes only a few months after they were married. The others died either of illness or in hunting accidents, so the story that she murdered them came later. Lady Mary was plain unlucky to have lost all those husbands.

Maybe the ghost sitting in that skeleton carriage is not her at all, but her father, disguised as a woman. You never know, with ghosts.

CHAPTER 26

Haunted Woodlands

OVER ON ANOTHER PART OF DARTMOOR, NEAR TWO BRIDGES, IS another haunted place, or so I've heard tell. It's a place called Wistman's Wood, and it is a truly magnificent woodland. It's very, very old, the oldest wood in Devon, and goes back to prehistoric times, would you believe. It once covered the whole of the West Dart Valley, from the Ice Age to the first settlements of prehistoric man. Now, do you know, I can't tell you how happy that makes me, that such a woodland is still around. After all these years! It's full of gnarled old oak trees all twisted up in a strange and eerie way, with moss and lichen everywhere. Trees that old and twisted must have taken hundreds of years to grow.

You can see why stories have grown around Wistman's

Wood. There were ancient tales about dragons there, in later tales, changed to reptiles – huge, writhing and hissing poisonous adders. There're stories about Druids having magic rites and rituals there, and charming the adders, making them harmless, with a magic rod made from a branch of a special ash tree.

There are also the Wisht hounds that haunt those woods. This is a pack of jet-black dogs, fierce ones, that roams around on misty nights jumping out at unsuspecting travellers.

I suppose anything that's as old as that woodland is bound to have many tales attached to it!

We've got some wonderful old woodlands in Exmoor too. One of these is Horner Woods, one of the largest ancient oak woods in England. It's not far from Stoke Pero, and well known for all the marvellous lichen and fungi that grow there. Underneath the old oaks are holly shrubs, wood sorrel, hazel and hawthorn, among others. Lots of different birdlife too – the wood warbler, flycatcher and, nesting up in the tree tops, the crows and buzzards. The woods are full of wildflowers in the spring too, and a good place where you might spot some red deer at the woodland edge.

Dunster Forest is an amazing place too, right outside of Dunster, a handsome town with a castle on one end, and a yarn market built in 1609 on the other. There is a fine priory church, a tithe barn, and a medieval dovecote too. In the forest there are the remains of two Iron Age hill forts, and if you walk up Gallox Hill to Bat's Castle and there about, you can see the Bristol Channel.

Talking about Dunster makes me think of the old Obby Oss tradition that goes way back to long-ago times and happens there every year on 1 May. The hobby horse comes from Minehead to dance down the streets of Dunster. The tradition goes that the people of Minehead are woken up by the beating of loud drums. The Obby Oss, a wonderful creature, is a wooden frame covered with cloth with a painted horse's head, usually carried on the backs of a couple of men. It's covered in feathers, ribbons, plumes and whatnot, and makes its journey the few miles from Minehead to Dunster to prance around the streets there. Music follows it everywhere, drums and squeezeboxes or accordions. It's a fine old evening, and good fun for everyone.

In Minehead, the hobby horse is known as the Sailor's Horse, and some stories say he was first used to scare off the Danish invaders who used to raid the coasts. Other towns have Obby Oss celebrations too, and there are different stories about the way they began.

One legend is that the origins of our Exmoor Obby Oss came from a ghost ship that sailed into Minehead harbour centuries ago without captain or crew. Then there are the stories that the tradition is older than that, that it goes all the way to prehistoric times, when humans used to dress themselves as animals and paint their pictures on the walls of the cave. Do you know, I don't think it matters a darn which story you believe, as long as everyone, from the very old to the very young, enjoys the tradition and has a good time out on the town on Obby Oss night.

I was telling about some of the different woods we've got in the West Country, and now here's a story about one of them. It happened many years ago to a farm worker I know living out on a farm outside of Exeter. This man was called Simon, and the woodland I'm talking about is Haldon Forest, which was not far from his home.

Now, Haldon Forest is a huge place, around 3,500 acres I do believe, and in those days – I'm talking forty odd years ago, maybe even nearer to fifty! My goodness, how time goes on – it was a much wilder place than it is now. A big area of the forest was full of conifer trees, big and dark, the ground underneath full of pine needles. A perfect spot, Simon used to say, for having a bit of fun with his girlfriend, Maggie.

So every Saturday night, the two of them, after a night at a dance somewhere, would drive out to Haldon Forest in Simon's old Ford two-door sedan and park in the densest, darkest part of the forest. If it was a warm, dry night, they'd get out of the car and sit down on the pine needles; if not, they'd stay there in the car for a bit of snogging before Maggie had to get home.

Now, this happened one June, on a clear moonlit night without a breath of wind anywhere. Simon and Maggie had been out on the razzle, for it was Midsummer's Eve, and there was not only the local pub to go to but a party somewhere afterwards. They left the party early, though, to go to their favourite spot in the forest for their usual bit of fun before Simon had to take Maggie back to her parents' home.

They'd got out of the car and were just settling down to a bit of hanky-panky when Maggie sat up sharply. 'Did you hear that?' she whispered into Simon's ear.

Simon, understandably, was reluctant to take his attention away from the matter at hand. 'Not a thing,' he said.

'Just listen for a minute. I'm sure I heard something.'

'Most likely 'tis an owl.'

Maggie sat up straighter, as alert as an animal sensing danger. 'There!' she cried. 'Can't you hear it now?'

Simon leaped up, because now he heard the sound that had frightened his girlfriend. It was the sound of horses' hooves, hundreds of them! And hollering, too, like a whole army of madmen was racing towards them on galloping horses.

God Almighty, can you imagine his fright? Maggie had heard them when they were still far away, but now they were coming closer.

The two of them ran to the car, slammed the door, tried to drive away, but Simon couldn't find the key. He wasn't about to go back outside and look for it in the pine needles, because those hoof beats were getting closer and closer. 'It sounded like bluddy thunder,' Simon said later, telling of it. 'I ain't never heard a sound like it before in my whole life.'

The windows were wide open in the car because of the warmth of the night – it was midnight by now – and Simon and Maggie were too terrified to close them. They huddled together, hoping and praying that the galloping horses would go around the car and not trample them to death. It sounded like the horses were heading straight towards them, and the noise was fearsome. As they sat there, cowering and shaking with fright, they heard the horses' hooves roaring right up to them, then around them and over them. 'And right through the bluddy car,' Simon said, 'as if we weren't bluddy there at all.' The sounds of shouting and hollering were deafening, but it wasn't till later, when they got over their fright, did they realize it sounded foreign, not like English at all. Not the English they knew anyway.

Then the sounds slowly died away as the phantom horses galloped into the forest.

For that's what they were – ghost horses. Because, do you know, Simon and Maggie didn't see a thing. Not one horse, not one rider. There was nothing at all – just the dark trees, the moonlight,

To this day, neither one of them has ever been back to that forest. Since then, Simon has heard tell of other woodlands in Devon where people have heard similar sounds, of an army on horseback. 'I think t'was them Romans,' Simon told everyone he met, for years. 'There was a Roman fort in Exeter all those years ago and there must have been many a battle with the natives. I'm sure what Maggie and me heard that night was the phantoms of those pesky Romans charging through the woods.'

He's an old man now, Simon is, but he still tells the tale to anyone who'll listen. Oh, and he married Maggie not long after. Her folks were that mad at the hour Simon got her home that night of the thundering hooves that they wouldn't let her out with him again. Of course, they didn't believe a word of their story about a ghost Roman army. So he had to marry her. As far as I know, they're still married, telling their great-grandchildren about the horsemen in Haldon Forest.

CHAPTER 27

Magic Adders

UP ON EXMOOR, THERE'S A PLACE CALLED HEALEY MILL. I WAS UP there not long ago with my camera, hoping to get some photos of a couple of hares I've seen around there. I didn't end up seeing the hares this time, but I saw a good many whortleberry bushes. I was so happy to see that they're still there. When I was still a boy, I'd go up to Healey Mill with my mum and dad and sisters, and we'd all pick whortleberries, all day long, selling them to get a bit of money. There was a small shop in South Molton that took all the whorts we could find, which was a blessing, as we made quite a bit from them every summer. We went everywhere, got to know all the best places to find those berries, places no one else could find.

We got to be great pickers, and I've known my dad to

pick as many as 32lbs of them in one day. Imagine, in just one day! D'you know how small those whortleberries are? Smaller than blueberries even! But he could pick them, my dad. And the bushes were loaded with them in those days. He had a secret weapon, though, a whort-picker that he made from a square tin with lots of prongs in it. He picked hundreds of those little buggers with his whort-picker. I'd never seen anything like it, and nothing since.

I'll never forget the day, years later, when I went out with Julie and her mother, up to Healey Hill to do some whortleberry picking. It was another fine day, late summer, and Julie's mum had brought a picnic for us to eat after we'd done our picking. Julie and her mum were going to make jam with the whorts, so we'd planned to pick a whole lot of them that day.

We put the picnic in the shade of a scrub oak and set off picking in the woods. The bushes were loaded, and they were good, fat whortleberries. The sky was a deep blue, and a couple of buzzards circled above us. We could hear their cry as we set off picking, spreading out to get the best ones. We had a container each, and when they were full up we brought it back to our big basket under the scrub oak and emptied them into it.

It was very hot that day, I remember. There wasn't a breeze to be had in the woods. I was picking those whorts one by one, all by hand and careful-like. If you did it like that, you never had to go picking them over and sorting them out later, which was a blessing for Julie and her mum.

So there I was, picking away, pleased as can be, because my container was just about full and I could go over to the oak tree, put them in the basket. Maybe have a drink of cold beer or cider that I hoped was in the cool box Julie had brought. The heat made it hard work. Even in the shady woods it was boiling that day.

I picked the last whortleberry, put it in my container and then yelped, 'Bledy hell!' A wasp had got inside my ear. I leaped up and swatted at my head, trying to get it out, the container of whorts flying out of my hand and the berries going everywhere. I'd lost the whole lot, but I didn't give a damn about that then. The wasp had stung me. I shouted and hollered, doing a war dance as I waved my arms, trying to get that wasp out.

Julie and her mum came running, thinking all sorts of dreadful things had happened to me. When they saw me leaping about, cursing about a wasp, they couldn't help laughing. Those women laughed and laughed, and I got madder and madder, until finally I calmed down and saw the funny side.

There was nothing for it but to pick up my container and start again. I went back to the whortleberry bush where I'd been picking, and was about to start again when I gave another shout. There, sitting on top of that bush, was the biggest adder I'd ever seen. It was staring at me as if daring me to pick even a single whort.

Me and that adder, we eyed each other. Now, adders don't attack unless provoked, but I didn't know how this one would feel if I brushed it aside to get at those berries.

Maybe that would be a provocation? I didn't think it was a good idea to tempt it, anyway. Though adder bites are usually mild, they are still poisonous, requiring immediate medical treatment. It probably wouldn't kill me, but I could end up feeling a bit rough for a few days.

Besides, it looked so comfortable there, sitting in the sunlight. It wouldn't take kindly to being moved. It must have been feeling lazy and lethargic, for it didn't slither away. This one was a brownish colour with a dark red-brown zigzag going down its back, so it was a female. The males are grey, and their zigzag marking is black.

I backed off, deciding to let the creature sit right where he was, on those whortleberries. That was it. I gave up. 'I'm packing up for the day,' I told Julie and her mum. They didn't blame me. They didn't like the idea of adders sitting on the whortleberry bushes either. So we went home with what we had, which was enough for Julie's mum to make an apple and whortleberry pie with anyway. And what a treat that was too. We sat in the garden and ate the pie with a great dollop of cream, enjoying every mouthful.

I never went back to Healey's Mill to pick whorts since that time. It's a shame, because it was a good place, and probably still is. Maybe this year some of the others in the family will have a go there, my granddaughters maybe. I'll warn them about the dangers, though. Wasps and adders – it's enough to put you off whortleberries for life!

*

Adders are the only poisonous snake we've got in England. They're not very long, never over 60cm, even though they're a stocky sort of snake. There are all sorts of old wives' tales about adders, most of them untrue. For example, years ago, they said female adders swallowed their young to protect them. Another belief was that adders didn't die until sunset. Neither of these is true, nor is the myth that adders hypnotize people with their stare. I suppose it's their unblinking eyes looking at you that give folk that impression.

In the ancient legends, the poor old adder is blamed for the death of King Arthur or, leastwise, starting the battle that killed him. The king and his men were on the battle-field, facing the armies of Mordred, the king's enemy. An adder suddenly came on to the field, and one of Arthur's men drew his sword and killed it dead. Mordred thought that the man had raised his sword to signal an attack, and so he charged.

I don't know if the king and his army weren't exactly ready to start fighting, or what, but Arthur lost his life in that fight.

Maybe this is why it was thought to be bad luck in old times to cross the path of an adder. In some places in the West Country, an adder on the doorstep was a terrible omen. Someone in the house would die, for sure. In other places, it wasn't so drastic. The snake would have to get into your house, and then someone would die within the year, not immediately. So you had a bit of time, I suppose, to get rid of the adder's spell, if it was possible!

Even dreaming about adders was not a good thing. It meant your enemies were on the move, scheming and plotting your downfall. So what you did was hang an adder skin above the fireplace, to bring good luck. It was also supposed to protect the house from fire. The adder had some good things said about it as well as bad. The adder skins were said to be very useful. They could cure rheumatism and suchlike, as well as headaches. They could also cure bites from the snake itself, so people thought many years ago. Folk said that, if an adder bit you, you had to catch it quick, slit it open and put the fat from under its skin on your wound, and it would heal. The trouble with that is that you'd probably get bitten several more times if you tried to pick up the adder.

Some folk even believed that, if you were brave enough to eat the flesh of the snake, you'd be able to speak the language of all the animals.

Even before all those tales about what adders could do, the snake was considered very important to the ancient people who lived in the south of Britain. To them, the adder was a symbol of a new start, of being born again. This was probably because snakes shed their skin regularly, so it seemed as if they were reborn each time.

From around this time, the time of the Celts, came the legend of the adder-stone. This was a kind of small stone which was said to have magical powers. They were worn around the neck of the people who had them, and were said to give them amazing perks. They could heal, and bring good luck in battle, and even make the owner invisible sometimes.

The story of how this stone was found is an odd one. In early spring, the legend goes, when all the adders came out after their winter hibernation, they met for a great battle, often on Midsummer's Eve. It lasted all night, those adders hissing and slithering and writhing, until dawn came. When they became exhausted and finally slithered away, they left a kind of green, frothy covering, all over the field they'd fought in. And in the middle of this stuff was a perfect polished stone, usually a sort of blue-green colour, small enough to wear around someone's neck.

It must have been some prize, to get this magic stone. I'm glad the adder had some good tales told about it, anyway.

CHAPTER 28

Cuckoos and Jackdaws

SO, I FINALLY GOT MY PHOTO OF THE CUCKOO. I COULDN'T believe how it happened, though. I'd been trying for weeks, ever since I first heard that cry this year – coo-coo, coo-coo – up to Anstey Common.

Now, I've got used to waiting hours to get a bird shot, but this cuckoo nearly had me beat. I tried everywhere, up on Molland Moor and Anstey Common, all over the place, where the cuckoo had been heard. I sat for hours with my camera outside Withypool, just sitting there, waiting. I could hear that bird calling but he bloody well wouldn't come into view. It was a beautiful spot, full of hawthorn trees all in blossom, but no cuckoo.

This went on for weeks. Then, the other day, my friend

Fred said to me, 'Johnny, I've never seen a cuckoo. Can you take me to see one?'

Like it was that easy! Now, Fred, he was a city man, as I've said before, so there were many sights he hadn't seen. I loved showing him the wonderful wildlife we have here in the country, and Fred loved seeing it. So I didn't have the heart to tell him how hard it was to see a cuckoo, even when you could hear it plain as day. 'Fred,' I said, 'I'll have a go, looking for a cuckoo with you, but you got to remember that it's a very shy bird. The chances are, we won't get a sight of it.'

'I know, Johnny, I know. Never mind. Let's give it a go. I've always wanted to see a cuckoo,' Fred said.

So off we went one morning. I thought I'd try up at Anstey Common first, as that was where I'd heard my first cuckoo this year, a few weeks back. It was a still morning, not a lick of wind. A thin white mist was hanging around down in the valleys, but the sun was burning off the edges. I said, 'Fred, let's find a place to sit and wait. I hope you're prepared for a long one.'

'Right, Johnny, I'm fine.'

'OK then. Let's go behind those gorse bushes over there.'

We started to walk towards the gorse, Fred off in front of me. Then – I still can't believe it! – a sodding cuckoo flew right out of a hawthorn tree right in front of Fred. That bird came so close he could almost have reached out to touch it!

Well, I had my camera ready and I got a shot of

that cuckoo. It was a one-in-a-million shot, let me tell you.

'Hey, Johnny,' Fred said later. 'I guess I bring you good luck, right?'

'Maybe you do, Fred,' I said, 'maybe you sure as hell do.'

We celebrated with a pint at the pub on our way home. It was a good morning for both of us that day. Fred had seen his first cuckoo, and I'd got my first photo of one.

The cuckoo was an important bird in times gone by. Farmers relied on hearing the cuckoo to tell them when spring had truly arrived. This was before the time of calendars, so that special sound the bird makes was greeted with great celebration. They had cuckoo festivals all over England, with much merrymaking and giving thanks that the winter was over and that they had survived it. The last one was in Cornwall. This was held at the end of April, when the cuckoo usually arrived.

There was once a Cornishman who really hated winter. He was old and felt the cold like nobody else, and he couldn't wait until spring arrived. One year, there was a terribly hard winter. There was snow and ice, and high winds and sleety rain, and it just went on, and on, and on.

The man couldn't take it any more. One Sunday, a bitter wind from the north-east was blowing around his house, with the temperature dropping even lower and the hailstones raining down on his room, and it was all so miserable that he decided, the hell with it. He would have his own festival to celebrate spring, even though there wasn't a sign of it yet.

He told a neighbour or two when they called by to see how he was, and though they thought he was a bit barmy, throwing a spring party when the season hadn't arrived yet, they told others in the village, like he'd asked them to. No one minded a good party, and they knew the old man had a good supply of drink in his cellar, and food tucked away in his larder. So all the villagers, every last one of them, showed up for this party.

Well, there they were, all crowded in the house, feeling quite cheery despite the wintry weather, except for the old man, who was still grumbling about spring being so late. He'd laid a huge fire in his big old stone fireplace and started to light it, to warm up his guests and get the party going. But to everyone's surprise, as he started to light the fire, a cuckoo flew out of a hollow log in the fireplace!

The bird flew around the room once, and then out the door, which had just been opened as more friends arrived. And do you know, as soon as that cuckoo got outside, spring arrived! The hail stopped, the wind dropped, and the temperature rose so high that everyone took off their woolly clothes and ran outside to welcome spring. It was a perfect summery day, and they ended up having the party outside, because it was too nice to stay indoors.

And that's what they were celebrating, down in Cornwall, for many, many years – that old man and the way he got spring to come by releasing the cuckoo from the hollow log.

*

I was thinking about that photo I finally got of the cuckoo as I was driving up Winsford Hill a day or so later, because Winsford was one of the places I'd sat in wait for the bird. As I looked out over the moor, I remembered the story I heard as a lad about the devil climbing up the very same hill and being tired after a night's work. I never did hear tell of what his work was that night, but it was bound to have been mischievous now, wouldn't it! Anyhow, the devil was completely whacked after his night out on the razzle, and plonked himself down, horns and tail and all, on the top of Winsford Hill, for a sit-down.

Next thing was this devil felt a great thirst coming on. Being a lazy sort of chap, he couldn't be bothered to go to the river for a cool, fresh drink of water. There being no pubs handy up there on Winsford Hill, he grabbed his spade, took out an enormous shovelful of dirt and scooped out a whole area of the moor, making a huge basin, a bit like a giant's soup bowl. Down in the bottom was a small stream, where the devil was able to drink his fill.

That hollow is still there, and it's known as the Punch Bowl. The Punch Bowl is a steep valley or gorge of 560 feet deep, and it's quite a sight. That wasn't the only landmark the devil made that night – when he dug his valley in one huge shovelful, he slung the dirt over his shoulder, where it landed a few miles away and became another famous Exmoor landmark – Dunkery Beacon, the highest point on the moor.

It's a wild and beautiful area, around the Punchbowl and Dunkery, full of steep hills and crevices, covered with gorse which seems to flower all year round, and vast patches of heather which, in the autumn, is spectacular. On Winsford Hill, surrounded by high, thick gorse, is a standing stone. It looks like any of the other standing stones dotted around Exmoor or Dartmoor, but this one has a name. It's called the Caractacus Stone, and it dates back to the fifth century, when the Romans occupied Britain. It's thought to be a memorial to the Celtic chieftain who led the first rebellion against the Romans, for the name Caractacus is carved into the stone.

Now that stone stayed in one spot until the 1930s, a long old time. But sometime around then – I think it was 1936, but I'm not exactly sure – disaster happened. That stone that had stood there all those years was found one morning lying on its side. You can imagine how shocked and horrified the local folk were, to come across this one morning.

The stone itself wasn't touched, wasn't defaced or any such thing, so it was obvious that whoever did it was after the treasure said to be buried there. An old Exmoor legend had told of this treasure, but no one took much notice of it, mind. I think the would-be thieves gave up after dislodging the stone and having a little dig around, as there wasn't much of a hole around it. If the buggers had been gravediggers they'd have known how to dig a proper hole, believe me!

The stone was undamaged anyway, and that was the main thing. The locals dug it up and moved it further from the road, where it still stands today in a very small stone building on Winsford Hill.

I was back at South Molton market again this morning, like I am every Thursday morning, at my stall, selling my photos, books and DVDs. It was a busy morning – not only all the local folk, but many visitors. It's June now, after all, and the tourists are starting to come down. A lovely man from up country bought a photo I'd taken only that morning, up at our land. I'd got up just after four and was out there as it was getting light, checking up on my cameras in the bird-boxes.

I was relieved that everything seemed fine on the land. No disasters like finding all the blue-tit chicks dead one morning a couple of weeks back. It was that hot spell we had in May, a week or so of boiling sun. I lost all my blue tits in that heat, and it broke my heart. Last year we had seven chicks, and they all survived. This year, there were nine eggs in the nest. Seven of them hatched, all lively and sprightly things, and within twenty-four hours they were all dead.

These things happen, but other things make up for it. A wren has made a nest in the badger house and is raising a couple of chicks there. They do make their nest in odd places sometimes. I've told before about the one nesting in a jug by the wall of our house once. I've also heard tell of a wren making a nest in a man's hat. He'd left it outside overnight by mistake. It was tossed into a wheelbarrow with some logs in it, to go inside for his wood-burner.

Next time he looked, a tiny wren was sitting there in his battered old brown cap looking up at him. He was a kind man and let the bird alone, even though it meant he couldn't use that wheelbarrow for weeks while the wren raised her one chick. He got that stressed too, worrying about cats and foxes and owls and other predators. 'Daft bledy bird,' he'd mutter to anyone who came to his place. 'Stupidest place I ever did hear of, nesting in a wheelbarrow. Anything could get it. Worries me to death.'

He got so concerned about that tiny wren and her baby that he got some thin fencing wire and put it up around the wheelbarrow every night, to keep them safe from predators. I don't know if it would've worked for a determined fox or even a tomcat, but whatever – the wren and her chick survived. That farmer tells the story to this day, and it happened some years ago. He's that proud of having protected that wren and her family. As I said, he was a good man.

I was thinking about that story as I checked my own wren's nest in the badger hide. I took a last look at the pond, and blow me if there wasn't a heron standing there, still as a statue. I had my still camera ready so I took a photo, and that's the one I sold this morning at South Molton market. I came home, printed it out, put it in one of the frames I keep in my office, and was in the market, with Julie, by eight in the morning.

Busy days, as I've said, but I love it. I love the long

daylight hours, and this time of year with all the nesting and birthing going on.

And talk about nesting, I was starting to tell about this farmer from Exmoor who was telling me an old tale at the market this morning. 'Johnny,' he said, 'you wouldn't believe what I saw a week or so back. You just wouldn't believe it.' He shook his head. 'You wouldn't believe it, Johnny,' he said again.

'Bill,' I said, 'how d'you know if I'll believe it or not if you don't tell me?'

He laughed, thought that was the funniest thing he'd ever heard. He's got a big, booming laugh, does Bill, and pretty soon half the folk in the market were gathering around to hear what was up. 'Well,' said Bill, 'there I was, up on my farm, checking out some sheep. I was leaning on the Land Rover, looking out over the pony paddock, and you'll never believe what I saw.'

By this time, there were more than half a dozen people openly listening to the story. Bill went on, 'There were two jackdaws perched on one of my ponies. Not one, but two, one on the top part, on its mane, the other down on its lower back. The one on the top was pulling hair out of the pony and stacking it on its back. Neat like, too, in little piles, like faggots of wood. Y'know what I mean, Johnny?'

I knew all right. I'd seen jackdaws do that before, pull the hair out of a horse's back for their nest. We had a deer, Bambi, that we raised, that I've mentioned before. Julie used to stand at the kitchen window and watch this jackdaw pull the hair from Bambi, worried that it was hurting, though Bambi didn't seem fussed.

But I didn't see a jackdaw make piles of the hair on the creature's back, and I said this to Bill. 'No, nor had I before this. That jackdaw made his little pile of faggots and then – this is what I could hardly believe even though I saw it with my own two eyes – the second jackdaw, the one sitting on his back, picked up the pile and flew away with it.'

Now that is some story. Bill was right, I could hardly believe it. The two of them, working together like that. But he'd seen it with his own eyes, and he's an honest man.

The more I work with nature, the more amazed I am about the wonder of it. The earth we live in is a truly wonderful place and I'm grateful every day to be part of it all.

CHAPTER 29

A Lovely Lady, and Some Badger Tales

I HAD A VERY SPECIAL VISITOR AT THE SOUTH MOLTON MARKET today too. It was the Exmoor writer Hope Bourne. She is ninety-two now, a very frail lady, her white hair pulled back with three simple slides, her face full of kindly wrinkles. She has lived on Exmoor for over sixty years and, for many of these, she lived in a leaky caravan at Ferny Ball, a few miles from Withypool. Through most of her life, she lived on the land. Her food was the animals she shot and the vegetables she grew herself; the fish she caught, too. The only money she earned was by helping out farmer friends now and again, but she didn't need much. Her biggest spending was on cartridges for her guns.

Hope Bourne taught herself many things, like drawing and painting. She began to write in a diary and wrote a book, *Living on Exmoor,* which was published in the early 1960s. She wrote other books too, as the years went by, and had articles published in local newspapers. She loved Exmoor with all her heart and walked all over it, for miles every day, with her sketchpad and notebook.

She hasn't lost that love for the land. And today at market someone had brought her in to see me. 'I wanted to meet you, Johnny,' she said, taking my hand and holding it for quite some time. It was like holding a small, delicate bird. She went on, 'I wanted to meet you because you feel the same for Exmoor as I do. If it wasn't for you and me, Johnny, Exmoor wouldn't be what it is.'

We were sat there for ages, like that. I told her what an honour it was meeting a fine lady like herself: 'You are a wonderful woman. I've always called you the Lady of the Moor. You have done so much for Exmoor.'

She told me that I had too, and that was why she wanted to meet me, to talk to me. She told me how special Exmoor was to her, and how it was up to folk like us to make people aware of what a wonderful, special place it is. 'So it doesn't get spoiled, Johnny.'

I know what she meant. Exmoor has always been a wild place, home to the ancient herd of red deer, but also to much more wildlife. It's full of such wonderful contrasts, from the windswept moorland covered in gorse and heather and wild grass to all the hidden woods and valleys. There are bogs and rushing rivers, and gentle streams going through bluebell meadows and mossy banks. There is so much here that must be cared for and saved, for our children and theirs.

God bless Hope Bourne, for all she's done in writing about Exmoor and keeping its spirit alive!

When she'd gone, I was very moved. I'd known all about her in the past, of course, but I'd never talked to her like this. I knew how she lived on the land for a pound a week, which was hardly anything, even in the old days. She had no running water but got drinking water from the streams and rivers. She picked food from the hedgerows and shot birds and small animals. She was truly amazing, and I thank the good Lord for giving us the chance to have a heart-to-heart talk at last.

I have a sad note to add here. After finishing this book, I heard that Hope Bourne passed away, on 22 August 2010. Rest in peace, Hope Bourne, and thank you for all the kind things you did for Exmoor.

I had a shock today on our land. I've been filming some swallows in my tepee for weeks. Now, I've got a colour camera in there, with cables going into the generator in the cabin where the monitor is set up. I've been watching these swallows closely on my monitor and was excited to see that these looked like rare birds. Unlike normal swallows, the pair in my tepee didn't have red throats. Also, one of them had a kind of white diamond shape on its head.

I put another camera in there so there were two on those swallows all the time. They had five eggs and hatched them all out. I kept looking and looking at these swallows. I'd never seen swallows looking like that before. No one else had either. I was telling people about them, and others came to have a look at the birds through the monitor. They all agreed that this was a rare type of swallow, so far unidentified.

I notified the BBC in Bristol, and they sent some people to look at it, along with people from the bird society. They were to come to our land the next week, to have a look at those rare swallows.

But that's when I got the shock. I was looking at the monitor from the second camera, and what could I see but a pair of normal-looking swallows! I couldn't believe my eyes. It turned out that the colour films had got it wrong. I didn't know it could happen. The colour was usually perfect in those films. I'd tested it again and again. It was so good it got the exact colour of everything, from different shades of flower and tree leaves to the tattoos on my arms.

But it had got the colour of those swallows wrong. The second camera was showing them to have red breasts, like normal swallows. And the white diamond – well, it was no more than a blip on the camera.

I made some phone calls pretty damn quick. All those people eager to come up and see those rare birds! I had to put them off, tell them what had happened. It was a lesson to me, though. The next day at the Royal Cornwall

Show, where I was giving a talk, I said what had happened to me. 'Don't always trust colour photography,' I told them. 'I was sure as hell fooled by it.'

Getting bird shots is an exciting part of my work. One of my favourite times was when I was with my friend and neighbour Fred and I found the peregrine. It was nesting in a disused quarry, 130 feet high on the cliff. Fred and I spent hours, waiting and watching from about three-hundred-odd feet away. The peregrine is a beautiful bird, large and powerful. Watching it fly is something else. It's so big, but it's fast, graceful. I got some helluva good shots, let me tell you. I got one of that peregrine coming in with a rabbit, and another time with a pigeon.

Fred and me, we kept a close watch on that bird for days. Even from that distance I spotted an egg in the nest with my binoculars. I was hoping to get some long-range photos of the chick when it hatched. But nature had other ideas. There were these great trees hanging over the quarry, the branches coming down near the nest. One day while Fred and I watched, we saw two squirrels run down a branch and, the next thing, the egg was gone. Nicked by the squirrels. It was a big disappointment, but that's the way it goes, that's nature.

It's like the badgers. I love the creatures. As I said, I even built a badger house on our land for them. I'd hate to see them die out but, even so, I think it was wrong for the government to make badgers a protected species thirty years ago. Nature would have sorted out the numbers in her own way, without interference. The sick ones, the ones with TB that the farmers quite rightly worry about, would have died or been killed. I know farmers who have lost all their cattle to TB from infected badgers that they couldn't touch because of the protected-species label. What's happened is that some farmers get rid of the badger setts illegally, whether the badgers are healthy or not, because they're not allowed to cull the sick ones.

My Uncle Arthur loved badgers. This was years ago, when I was a lad still in Braytown. He and Auntie Nora lived in the village, in a little bungalow at the edge. For years, Uncle Arthur had a tame badger he reared from a baby. He used to walk him around on a lead. He loved wild animals, used to fall in love with so many of them. He raised a baby fox too, as well as wild rabbits and suchlike.

The funny thing was, Uncle Arthur ate badger meat as well. In those days, you could love animals but you couldn't afford to be sentimental over them if you wanted to eat. I had my first taste of the meat from Arthur. 'Badger ham, Johnny,' he said as he gave me a slice off the back legs. It was quite tasty, if I remember rightly.

Uncle Arthur used to trap the badgers to sell the skin; they were used for the bristles in shaving brushes. He taught me how to do it. He was good to me. He taught me how to box as well, but I've talked about that in my other book. I had a lot of time for my Uncle Arthur.

He told some good stories – all true ones. He knew a couple of chaps, two brothers, who were trapping badgers in a big way. They made good money out of the skins. One night, they were in the pub and, before long, they were pie-eyed. As they went out to the car, parked by a wood next to the pub, they saw a badger. It must have been sleepy or under the weather or something, for they managed to take it by surprise and killed it outright.

It was a fair old size, and they were over the moon, thinking they'd earned themselves a bit of cash to cover their beer money that night. They chucked the dead badger in the boot of their car and drove it into the garage where one of the brothers lived. They had all the knives ready in the garage; they'd done this a hundred times before.

They got everything ready, knives and all, and opened the boot of the car to get that dead badger out. They got one hell of a surprise instead. The badger jumped out at them, snorting his head off. It ran like crazy, going round and round the garage, and those two jumped up on some boxes to get out of its way.

Those men were as stunned as the badger had been, for they never killed it but knocked it out for a bit. It had come to, fighting for its life. It got away, because the brothers were too full of drink to get over the shock quick enough. The garage was an old wooden one with a wobbly door that didn't fit properly, and that badger ran out of there, free as can be.

Uncle Arthur always said to me, when he told this story, 'I'm bloody glad that creature got away, Johnny. It deserved to live, after being in that car. I'm surprised it wasn't killed off by the alcohol fumes.'

I loved that story. I'm glad that old badger lived too. He must've been one tough animal, to survive a blow on the head and two pie-eyed blokes coming at him with knives. His descendants would be welcome to come live in my badger house any day.

There was all sorts of folklore about badgers. Long ago, people believed that they had legs shorter one side than the other. That's because folk saw them walking around and about on hills quite often, so they naturally thought the legs on one side of their body had to be shorter.

Like the owl, there are some superstitions about badgers bringing good luck and some about bad luck. One of the bad ones is that if you hear a badger cry out right before an owl hoots, you've had it, mate. You are a dead man, that's for sure. That's what they thought, anyway.

If a badger crossed your path, though, that would bring good luck, just like if a black cat did. But with the badger, there was a catch. If the animal dragged its feet a bit as he was walking along in front of you, and happened to scratch up a bit of dirt – oh dearie me, you had better start getting your coffin ready.

Badgers were very important, though, for protection against witches. You had to get hold of the hair of a badger; one hair would do. The trickier part would be getting the skin of a black cat, to make a bag to put this badger hair in. If you did manage to do this, you could roam anywhere you like and be safe from the wickedest meanest witch that ever lived.

Not very nice for the cat, though, is it!

CHAPTER 30

Sacred Yew Trees

DO YOU KNOW, TO THIS DAY I CAN'T DRIVE PAST A CHURCHYARD without remembering a story from my old gravedigging days. It's in my blood. My father was a gravedigger, and so was I. And though I've written about these stories in other books, every village church I pass reminds me of a new tale.

Now, this story I'm telling you is one that's not been told before. You see, it happened to a very important family in our area. It was a long time ago, mind, or I wouldn't be telling of it now. But I'm still not naming names.

This woman who died was a fine lady, and a friend of mine. I was proud to be burying her ashes in the family gravesite. It was at one of the parish churches not far from Brayford. I did an extra-specially good job, digging the grave carefully for these ashes. Then I covered everything up good and fine and stood for a moment at the graveside, to pay my respects.

That was when I noticed my mistake. 'Oh shit,' I said to myself. I'd buried the woman in the wrong grave!

I said it out loud. 'What can I do?' I wanted so much to give this lady a decent burial. I'd been to the service for her at the crematorium, but because she was a friend I wanted to do this last thing for her.

And now I'd made a sodding mess of it!

After thinking for a minute or two, I went haring down to the village. I needed a bloke to help me out, someone who could keep quiet too. I didn't want to let this story get out, no way. The first person I came across was a man named Sean. 'Hey, Sean,' I cried. 'C'mon, mate, you gotta help me out.'

He followed me back up the hill to the churchyard. I explained what had happened. He agreed it was a disaster. 'But what'd'ya want *me* to do, Johnny? Help you dig up the ashes?'

'No, Sean, I can do that myself. What I want you to do, see, is to stand at the graveside as I dig her up and bury her in this grave right next to the wrong one. That's where she belongs. But I want to do it with respect, see? I want you to pretend you're the vicar and say some prayers while I lay her to rest.'

Now Sean, he was a good man, and understood why it was important not to dig a lady up without some ceremony. So he put on a solemn face and bowed his head and said a few prayers while I dug up the ashes and buried them all over again in the right grave.

When it was all over I took Sean to the King's Arms in South Molton and treated him to a jarful of cider. He promised me he'd not tell a soul about what we did, and do you know something? I believe he kept his promise. And anyone reading this, you keep it under your hat too, ha ha!

I suppose that's not the last graveyard story I'll remember. Next time I go to Molland and pass the church there, or at High Bray, or anywhere in that area, I'll think of another one. It's amazing how many stories you have to tell when you're a gravedigger.

One of the things you can't help noticing when you work in a churchyard is all the yew trees. Some of them are very old, so people must have been planting these trees around churches for centuries.

The yew tree has a long life, with long branches that can take root when they reach the ground. I've heard that some English yews are as old as four thousand years! That's some tree. This is probably the reason why they are planted around churches, for they are a symbol of eternal life.

The yew tree knows how to adapt, for sure. Any tree that old has to learn how to overcome climate changes, and all sorts of things. It has to be tough to survive. It's a slow-growing tree but is very resilient, very hardy.

But the yew is not just a nice tree growing in a church-yard. It is highly poisonous, so if you ever have to work with it, take very good care. All of it is poisonous: the bark, the wood, and even the needles and the seed.

So there was a good reason why, in the past, it was called the tree of death. In the Middle Ages, they used arrows tipped with poison made from the yew tree, so that shows you how dangerous the tree could be. All those long-ago people who carved tools and other things out of the wood of a yew tree had to be bloody careful!

There were many old tales connected with this tree. Long ago, the Celts thought it was sacred. It was the link between life and death. It was protection against evil spirits, and it was believed that the yew could connect a person to his dead ancestors. Later on, in Christian times, the yew was sometimes part of funeral services, when small branches of the tree were put either underneath or on top of the coffin. It came to stand for an everlasting life in heaven.

Would you believe, I just met another gravedigger, a man from Wales, called Joe, who was on my last safari. We spent hours exchanging stories. There was one he told me that really made me laugh.

Years ago, Joe had to dig a grave for a well-known opera singer. This woman was short and a bit hefty, so the grave had to be dug to certain specifications, the coffin being particularly short but wider than normal.

'The trouble was,' Joe told me, 'there was a small rock

about nine inches from the bottom that I couldn't dislodge. It just wouldn't move. Well, the time came for the
burial and, would you believe, the coffin got stuck on that
rock. The head of it just wouldn't go down. I tell you,
Johnny, that was a bad moment for me.'

'I know how you must have felt,' I said. 'I've had stuff
like that happen to me too. What in the hell did you do?'

'All I say is, thank goodness it was a Welsh funeral. You
know how us lot like to sing. And this was an opera star,
so there was a proper choir at the funeral, with a
conductor and all. I went over to him, had a quiet word.
The good man understood and turned the choir and all
the mourners in such a way that they weren't facing the
open grave. So there they were, singing their hearts out,
their voices booming through the valley and out over the
Welsh hills, while I tried to sort that coffin.'

Joe had his daughter with him at that funeral, helping
out as she sometimes did. The first thing he tried was
getting her to jump on the coffin to get it past that rock,
but it wouldn't budge. The vicar, standing waiting for the
singing to be done to go on with the service, saw that
the gravediggers were in a spot of trouble, and also
that some of the mourners were having a bit of a peep to
see what was going on. So there was another whisper
to the conductor who, in between songs, angled the choir
and everyone else even further so that their backs
were completely turned. He called out, 'Let the next
song ring out to the hills and valleys, so that our
dearly departed friend can be carried with it to heaven.'

'Just imagine it,' said Joe. 'There was this beautiful music belting out loud and clear and wonderful, out over the Welsh landscape, while there was I, stamping on that coffin to get it to go down properly.'

'Is that what you did?' I wanted to know.

'Yep. All seventeen stone of me! And I got it down. Yessir, I got it down before that singing was finished, and no one was the wiser.'

Oh, we had a right old time, that nice Welshman and me, remembering all the things that happened to us when we were gravedigging! I wonder if such things happen now, with all the machines and equipment they have these days for burials. Probably not. Life was haphazard in those old days, and so was death. It wasn't a bad thing sometimes, to have a good laugh at both now and again.

CHAPTER 31

The Beast of Exmoor

ONE THING I'VE NEVER GOT A PHOTO OF IS THE BEAST OF Exmoor. Now, that would be something! This beast has become a modern-day legend. Some swear it doesn't exist, that it's a particularly large cat or dog. But I know folk who have seen it, and I've heard its cry, so I know there's a beast out there somewhere. But as to exactly what it is, I'm no wiser than anyone. Those that have seen it say it looks like a huge cat, a puma or some such thing.

My wife, Julie, and my son Craig saw the cat one day. They were driving along the North Devon link road and saw a huge cat down on the bank. Luckily, they were going slowly, and there weren't any cars behind them. They backed up to have another look and the cat hissed at them. It definitely was far too big to be a domestic cat.

For me, it all started well over twenty years ago, after a farmer near South Molton had lost near about thirty sheep over a few month period. They'd all been killed in a violent way, their throats cut to shreds in a way no dog would have done. Their faces seemed to have been sliced from the ears downward. Some of the lambs had their ears completely torn off.

One night, this strange creature was sighted down our way, so the marines were called out. I was one of the guns that went along with the marines. A family claimed it had seen the beast go into a nearby wood, so off we went, hollering and shouting. My goodness, what confusion there was! Those marines were firing at gates and wooden posts, and I believe there was a stray dog or two that got shot, being mistaken for the beast. It was bloody chaos, let me tell you.

But no one managed to get whatever it was that was killing the sheep, and no one saw the big cat either. Maybe that was because everyone was busy looking at the ground, and no one thought to look up into the trees in that wood! The beast was probably looking down at us, swishing his long tail and having a right old laugh!

I got called out a few times when the beast had been seen. Someone spotted it on a railway line at 1 a.m. one night, so some of us met up at Drewston Lane, near South Molton. My mate and I had rifles, but we never used them. We didn't see anything but, suddenly, we heard horrendous noises and cries coming from the fields beyond. The sheep and lambs were making a hell of a row. Something had frightened the shit out of them.

I got called out many times to go and hunt the cat, but we never got it. Once, a man rang to say a strange animal was stalking a hind and calf. It was like no other animal he'd seen around these parts. Other people saw it too, that time, but by the time I got out there, it had gone.

One night, I was in the badger hide at Twichen when I heard a loud screeching noise. I'd never heard anything like it before, and haven't since. It put the fear of God up me, let me tell you. The next day, I found out that at least three farmers had heard the same thing. That was definitely the beast, for sure.

There has been all sorts of speculation about the creature. Some even think it might be a cross between a puma and a leopard. People have had glimpses of it but have never been close enough to identify it. One woman I met remembers that, when she was about ten years old and playing at a friend's house up on the moor, the children were suddenly called inside by the mother. They were told to stay inside the house with all the windows and doors shut tight while the mother phoned the police. Armed men came out straightaway but in the end never found anything. The girl, though, saw this big cat, about five foot long, black or dark brown, up in a tree near the window of the house. By the time she'd got the attention of the adults, the cat had gone. She's never forgotten it to this day, and that was about twenty years ago.

Someone else spotted the beast near Simonsbath, sitting at the edge of the river dipping his huge paw in, as if trying to catch a fish!

I'm sure there's been something out there; maybe there still is. We know now that people have kept wild animals as pets and have let them go when they got too big or too dangerous to handle. The beast could be one of those – who knows? – and if there was more than one, they might have bred. Maybe, if someone ever gets hold of one, we'll know for sure. For now, everyone likes a good mystery, and that's what the beast is – one that's not solved yet.

It's not just a puma-like cat that has been seen on the high moor ground. Not that many years ago, a group of schoolchildren saw a black bear-like beast around Hound Tor on Dartmoor. It was about the size of a small pony, with a thick, shaggy coat and very large, strong front legs, and looked as if it could tear an animal twice its size from limb to limb.

Someone, probably one of the schoolteachers with the children, took a photo of this creature which appeared in one of the national newspapers. It's bit blurry, but it does look like a shaggy cross between a wolf and a bear. Animal experts who saw the photo said it certainly wasn't an ordinary domestic dog.

Of course, many stories flew around that it was one of the hounds of hell that are supposed to haunt the area. These are demonic beasts who are said to be looking for a certain squire who sold his soul to the devil then went back on the deal. The hounds are looking for his grave, to dig him up and cart him off to hell. Their howls can be heard at night. This legend gave Sherlock Holmes the idea for his famous book *The Hound of the Baskervilles*.

Just as the wild hounds haunt the moors, so all sorts of sad spirits haunt houses around our way.

Up in Ilfracombe, there's said to be the oldest haunted house in England – Chambercombe Manor – though I suppose many old places make that claim. It seems a human skeleton was found in a secret room in the manor house. Turned out it was a female; maybe the owner's daughter. They say that, to this day, you can hear a moaning from that secret room sometimes, and her footsteps walking around the corridor.

The story is that a farmer living there found the skeleton. This was about a hundred and fifty years ago. He was doing some repairs on the thatched roof and noticed the outline of a window which had once been there. When he looked closely, he saw that the bricked-up window was not in any of the bedrooms but in a space between two of them. So he knocked down a wall and found something truly horrible. It was a beautiful old room, all hung with fancy tapestries and suchlike, but covered in thick dust. In the middle was a big four-poster bed, and on that bed the skeleton of a woman.

Now, the legend goes back to another two hundred years before the farmer's discovery. It seems a man called William Oatway came back to Chambercombe Manor to live, after being away for some time. It turned out that his father, a famous wrecker, had passed away, leaving many debts. This William did not share his father's profession; in fact, he didn't like the idea of wrecking very much. It was a nasty business, and went on for a long time along the different coastlines in the West Country, and other places, I'm sure. What happened was that certain greedy, wicked men would go out on the most dangerous rocks on dark, stormy nights, waving torches and lanterns when a ship was out there. If the sea was hazardous, the captain of the ship would be relieved to think that the lights were those of a safe harbour, leading him and his passengers to safety. But, instead, the ship would be wrecked on those treacherous rocks and, as it sank, the wreckers would jump on board and start looting. Many innocent people lost their lives at the hands of the notorious wreckers.

So this William Oatway, he didn't want to be a wrecker like his father but, you see, he was responsible for his father's debts. He realized that the only way he could repay them was to wreck and loot a ship. He decided he would do it once, and then never again.

So, on one fearsome, stormy night, with the wind howling and the waves higher than houses, William and his men lit their lamps and lured a ship on to the rocks. William was looting the damaged ship when he saw that one of the injured people on it was a woman. She was dressed in very fine clothes, but was hurt pretty bad.

Now, I don't know if William had a fit of conscience

and felt sorry for what he'd done, causing that boat to wreck on those dangerous rocks, but he decided to take the woman home secretly to Chambercombe Manor. There, he and his wife, Eleanor, tried to save her, but it was no good. The injuries she got in the shipwreck were too much for her, and she died without ever gaining consciousness.

But that wasn't the end of the story. It was later that day when the full horror of what he'd done hit William. He overheard talk in the town from sailors on another ship and, little by little, he pieced together a tragic story. The woman who died was his daughter, Kate. He hadn't recognized her because she'd married an Irishman and moved away with him many years before. She was on her way to visit her parents, and would have got there safely if her own father hadn't wrecked the ship she was travelling in.

Of course, William couldn't bury his daughter properly, for he would have been exposed as a wrecker, so he put her on the best bed in the house and walled her body in the secret room.

His wife died of grief soon after. William couldn't bear living in that place alone, knowing what was in that secret room, so he moved away to Cornwall. The story goes that his signed confession was found in the chimney of an old house in Fowey, around two hundred years later.

To this day, crying and sighs and footsteps can be heard in Chambercombe Manor. It was probably the daughter, Kate, killed in a shipwreck caused by her own father.

*

I was in Ilfracombe not all that long ago, and it was hard to imagine any ghost wanting to haunt the place, with the sun shining on the cliffs and the wonderful expanse of coastline, and the boats bobbing about in the harbour. But people love stories, and skeletons in closets are always good ones! There are so many tales that get passed down year after year, and have done for centuries, until no one knows where the story came from.

Like up in Lynmouth. Now, that's a beautiful place, still in Exmoor National Park but right on the coast. It's down in a 700-foot gorge, right below Lynton, another pretty place. There was a terrible flood in Lynmouth in 1952, in August. Exmoor was soggy already with a wet summer, and nine inches of rain fell in one day. All the floodwater came running over the moor. Dams were formed with uprooted trees, but they finally gave way, flooding the town. It killed over thirty people and destroyed more than a hundred homes.

Years ago, the sea at Lynmouth was full of herrings. The fishing boats came back loaded with them. But then, suddenly, sometime in the 1800s, all the herring dis-appeared. It was a real mystery. No one, not the fishermen, nor folk who studied the sea, could figure out why.

But the people of Lynmouth had their own ideas. Many blamed the local church. It had started charging a herring tax on the locals. You can guess that this didn't go down too well. There were clashes between the church and the people of Lynmouth; serious trouble.

So the herring, being peaceable-type fishes, decided to just up and leave. They couldn't bear to be responsible for all that conflict! They upped and left and never came back, and that's why there is no herring fishing at Lynmouth today.

If you don't believe that story, here's another tale for you. The story goes that there were so many herring the fishermen didn't know what to do with them. They and their families ate herring every night, and sold what they couldn't eat, but still there was a glut of the fish. So the locals used what they couldn't eat or sell for manure for their crops. D'you know, those herring were so insulted by that, they left in a huff and never returned.

CHAPTER 32

Burning Tar Barrels

I WAS THINKING THE OTHER DAY OF MR COWDRY, WHO WAS THE vicar of North Molton back in the days when I was gravedigging. He was also the reverend of Twichen and many of the small parishes where I dug graves, so I got to know him pretty well.

Now, every morning at nine o'clock, Mr Cowdry would ring the church bells. He'd ring them like he was calling in the faithful from all over Devon and Somerset. It wasn't a chore for him, it was an honour, I do believe, for that vicar to ring those bells.

Often, when he arrived at the church early in the morning, I'd be there already. I can still see him now. He had white hair and a rosy face. He was quite a sight, standing on a plank on the grass, right over me where I was digging the grave. After he had said good morning, and asked me how I was, he used to say, every time, 'And who are you moving today, Johnny?' or, 'Who are you throwing out there today, Johnny?' Then he'd say, 'Be careful where you put them, Johnny.'

Those who read my first book know what he was talking about. When you dug a grave in those crowded churchyards, where people were buried for years and years, you always came across other coffins or, more often, bones from folk dead longer than anyone could remember. A gravedigger has to be careful to juggle things about, make room for the new coffin.

So Mr Cowdry always asked, with a twinkle in his eye, 'So who are you chucking around today, Johnny?'

I'd stop my digging, look up at him with a grin and say, 'You go on back in your church, Vicar, and ring those bells, and then I'll tell you who I've moved today, when I get a bit deeper.'

And then I'd carry on digging, with the sound of the church bells going across the valley and out towards the hills. It was nothing much, our little exchange, no more than small talk to start our day. But it gave both of us some pleasure. And isn't this what life is all about anyway – all the little pleasures we get from it? Pile them all together and it adds up to a happy life.

When Mr Cowdry died, I made sure I found a prime place for him, right near the church door. It was a clean grave to dig, and I didn't have to move anything. He deserved it, did the reverend. He was a good man.

*

Talk about graves and suchlike makes me think of that small grave on Dartmoor, at a crossroad near Throwleigh and Gidleigh. It's called Jay's Grave, and a young maid called Kitty Jay is said to be buried there. She lived and died more than two hundred years ago.

Kitty Jay was an orphan, and grew up in the poor-house. When she was in her teens, she was sent to work on a farm near Manaton. It was hard work, as you can imagine. In those days, poor servants like Kitty had to work both in the house and out in the fields from early morning to late at night. They didn't get any wages, just a place to sleep and food to eat, which I guess meant a great deal to a poor girl like her.

Well, what happened to her must have happened hundreds of times. She was taken advantage of by the young man of the household and got pregnant. She was only sixteen years old, poor maid.

In those days, if a girl fell, it was all her own fault, never the man's – and especially a girl like Kitty, with no family or friends. She was turned right out of the house, without any place to stay or anyone to turn to. No one would help her, because everyone condemned her as a slut and would have nothing to do with her.

So she did what she probably thought was the only option open to her. She committed suicide. She was found hanging in the barn of the farmhouse.

In those days, a suicide couldn't be buried in consecrated ground, so she couldn't be buried in the churchyard. None of the villages wanted anything to do with the girl's body so, in the end, she was buried at the crossroads where three parishes intersect. This was not uncommon in those times. Both suicides and criminals were sometimes buried at crossroads, as no one wanted them in their churchyards.

The story would have ended there, and Kitty Jay would have been forgotten, if strange things hadn't started to happen at her grave. The first was that there were always fresh flowers on the grassy mound where she was buried. Nobody knew who put them there, and no one was ever spotted. This went on right up until modern times – till a few years back, anyway. I know of a few old Dartmoor farmers who, when they were lads, tried to catch the person who put the flowers on the grave. Some fell asleep, others say they were scared away by a ghostly figure wandering over the grave.

There are all sorts of stories about who it was that put the flowers on the grave. One tale says it's the ghost of the man who got her pregnant then abandoned her, his soul doomed to wander Dartmoor for ever for his sins.

I was talking to someone who lives near Kitty Jay's grave the other day, and he was telling me how, when he was a boy, fifty-odd years ago, the grave was just a story known to locals. All it was was a mound of grass, hardly anything more, with nothing there, only those few fresh flowers every day. But now, he says, it's become a big tourist attraction. It's in every guidebook on Dartmoor. Jay's Grave is covered in plastic flowers, coins, trinkets, little gifts – all sorts of stuff. The people come from every-where to queue up to take photos of themselves on the poor girl's grave.

It's strange, isn't it? All these years, Kitty Jay's grave was in the middle of nowhere, hardly known to anyone, and now it's become some kind of shrine for tourists. I wonder if she'd be pleased, or just bewildered? Poor girl probably needs to just rest in peace, I would imagine. I hope she is. But some people say she's not, for her ghost has appeared often around the burial spot. A girlish figure with a hood has been seen standing dejectedly on the grave. Another spirit appears on moonlit nights, kneeling on the grave with his head in his hands. Some folk think this is the ghost of the man who was the father of Kitty's child, now repentant and weeping for the loss of his child and the child's mother. Others think it is one of the men who hounded her after she was thrown out of the farmhouse, drove her to suicide.

Whatever you believe, it's certainly one of the oldest and most well-known legends of Dartmoor.

The ghosts that appear on Jay's Grave seem harmless, but there are other, more dangerous ghosts on Dartmoor. Not that far from Kitty Jay's resting place is a kind of valley, or cleave, up on the moor, a favourite place for walkers. Once, though, a few years back, a woman was walking her dog down the cleave when, suddenly, she was filled with a terrible feeling of dread. She'd gone that way many a time, and nothing had happened like this! She stopped, frozen, and so did her dog, who seemed as terrified as she was.

Then a horrible sight appeared. Out from behind the rocks and stones of the cleave came these tiny figures, all hunched and ragged and looking quite evil indeed, with their dark clothes and horrible, scowling faces. The woman nearly died of fright. Her dog started howling, such a terrible howling that, later, the people down in the village heard him and started to go looking for the woman. But before they could get to her, she'd managed to turn and run away from the strange figures, whoever or whatever they were. The woman was in a right state, crying and trembling and fearful. The women of the village tended to the woman, who was nearly dead of fright, while the men bravely went up to where the woman had seen the weird creatures. There was nothing there, but the men swore later that there was a frightening atmosphere, along with a foul smell, a mixture of something burning and something rotting.

No one ever saw the figures after that and, to this day, nobody knows what or who they were. But people still say that there is a presence there, something dark and evil, and no one walks their dogs there any more. Even tourists who don't know the story find the place eerie. One or two have mentioned it in the village shop, and told how their dogs' hackles rose when they walked along the cleave. It sounds a place to steer clear of, if you ask me!

*

It's hard to think of anything dark and frightening on a beautiful spring day on Exmoor, like we've had these last few days while I've been filming. But things are different in the winter months. And in those old days before electric lighting, when the nights were long and bitterly cold and the days foggy and freezing, you can understand the thinking of folk long gone by. And you can understand why they had all these customs to scare away the evil spirits they believed were hiding in the darkness.

In Devon, many towns have some kind of a festival in autumn, usually around November, to rid their village of these malign spirits. There's a place called Northlew, in West Devon, where they say the devil died of cold, and every year there's a procession around the village where a burning torch is held up to scare away old Satan. I'm sure this takes place, in one way or another, in other villages as well, like it's been doing since old times.

Another thing they used to do in Devon, until it got a bit dangerous and Health and Safety stepped in, was to roll a burning barrel down the main street of the town. I believe this custom may still be happening in one or two places, or was until recently anyway.

This burning-barrel story goes way back to the seventeenth century, would you believe! In Ottery St Mary, in Devon, there is not one burning barrel, but up to seventeen! They don't roll them down the main street, though, they carry them. This is what happens. Each pub has its own barrel, which is soaked in tar. On the big day, they are lit one at a time. The women and children get to carry a smaller barrel in the afternoon and early evening, but it's later on when the real fun starts.

It's the men's turn to carry the barrels, and some of these weigh up to 60 or 70 pounds. That's some big flaming barrel, let me tell you. The town gets packed with people, all having a high old time, everyone wanting to get a bit of the action, getting as close as possible to the burning barrels or having a chance to carry one through the town.

The barrels finally end up at the edge of the River Otter, where they go on a huge bonfire. By then, all the hollering and fun and burning flames have got rid of all the evil forces lurking about at this dark time of year. That was the belief all that time ago, and that's why the tradition is still carried on. Folk might not believe much in the devil and evil spirits these days, but it's always good to hedge your bets! And why not? It's a great night out on the razzle, as those who have been there will tell you.

CHAPTER 33

A Floating Hide

THE FILMING OF BIRDS FOR THE NEW BBC4 SPECIAL IS GOING full swing now, and life is busier than ever. After leaving our land the other day, I went to the woods where me and Tony used to stand, watching the badgers. I got a camera set up there too, and did I get a surprise when I had a look. Two chicks had hatched out! I was over the moon. The mother owl was sitting there, so I only got a tiny glimpse of a bit of fluff and whatnot, but that was enough for me to see what was there. I can't say enough how happy I was when I saw that. I kept thinking of my mate Tony, how excited he would be, seeing those chicks in his hide. Tony, me old friend, I hope you're having a good look down here, seeing what's going on in that old hide of ours. I wish you were here with me, that's for sure.

When I got back home, I told Julie all about it, and she was as thrilled as I was. Then, as we were having a cuppa, we started talking about some of the other old hides I had in the past. They were always on someone else's land, before I had land of my own. I'll always be grateful to the wonderful people who let me use their land to put up a hide. For many years I did that. The trouble was, so often either the land would be needed for something else or the folk who owned the land would sell it to someone else and, once again, I'd have to abandon my hide. Now I've got our own land, and it's a great feeling.

Anyhow, Julie and I were sat there drinking tea and remembering things. Some were good, some near disastrous, like when I was stuck in a floating hide. 'D'you remember that, Julie?' I asked with a laugh.

'How could I forget? I was frightened to death. I thought you were going to drown.'

The way it happened was this. I was working for a film company that wanted me to get some shots of wader birds. I tried very hard, but the shots weren't good. I just couldn't get close enough to the birds.

Someone in the film company had the clever idea – or it seemed so at the time – of rigging up a kind of raft or something that would float. The people up at Bristol, where the crew came from, sent me two lengths of polystyrene. It was light and would float, sure enough.

I looked at this stuff, wondering what the hell to do with it. 'I've got an idea,' I said to Craig, my son. 'Let's make a floating hide.'

274

I thought it was a fantastic idea. I could get out there and be near enough to the birds to get some bloody good shots. 'Let's get going,' I said, and off we went, making this floating hide.

Craig and I worked for about a week on it. Some parts were filmed. The crew got a laugh because, to save time, I even got them to work, hammering away. It looked very funny on the finished film.

We were pleased with our floating hide when it was done. The next thing we had to do was to test it. Our first trip was to go up on the north coast of Devon to a place near Instow. What a job that was, getting it there. We set off from Bishops Nympton, through South Molton towards Barnstable, then on towards Instow, stopping at the Tarka Trail. From there, we had to carry the floating hide up the Tarka Trail. We got to the marshland and, from there, made our way on to the sandbank. It was hard work, going through that sludgy sand and dirty mud. My boots sank down deep, and sometimes it was bloody hard to pull them out. I got stuck several times, and didn't think I'd ever get moving again.

At last, I got on to a sandbank. There I had to sit and wait until the tide came and picked me up. The plan was to float downriver towards Barnstaple, to film some spoonbills.

It all sounded very well, but it was a damn silly and dangerous thing to do. The water was deep and running fast. I didn't think of the danger then, because I was filming like crazy. I got some nice pictures of the spoonbill.

But then I saw that the water was rising fast, and the wind was coming up something fierce. It was rough and scary out there, and I panicked. I tried to get back to where I set off from, but the water had risen so high I couldn't see the deep gully I'd crossed over. I had to cross it again to get back to shore, you see.

Luckily, the film crew had stayed in exactly the same spot on land where I'd left them. I could still see them, so that gave me an idea where the gully was. Thank God they were still there for, if they'd taken off, I wouldn't be here telling this story today. I'd still be out there floating on that darn hide! But everything went right after that – well, it did until the last bit, when I had to walk out of shot. I took four steps and got stuck in the mud. The crew laughed like hell. They kept filming, though, and it was on TV. People talk to me about that last shot still to this day. It was a good laugh.

After that, the crew wanted me to do some more filming with the floating hide. I said, 'No way.' I was not going down on that north coast again. I was lucky to get back, and I was not pushing my luck by having another go.

So, instead, I decided to try the Somerset levels. I knew I'd be all right there. There is no tide, for a start. And because we'd had a lot of rain the last few weeks, a lot of sea birds were on the waterlogged fields.

So off I went in my floating hide again. This was better; the water was only about three feet deep. It was a long way and, unfortunately, a very windy day. But I was lucky and got some very good shots of different kinds of birds. I felt pleased as the day finished and it was time to head back.

But there was trouble here too. Up on the levels, there were lots of deep gutters that had filled with water, many of them six feet deep. I got in one of these, and couldn't get out. Then – I could hardly believe it – my floating hide started to break up. I was scared shitless and started panicking again. I couldn't swim, I was in deep water and my hide was falling apart. The film crew was about 200 yards away from me, so they couldn't help. All they could do was watch me flounder about on my broken hide.

I just about managed to get out of there, don't ask me how. 'Never again,' I said to the crew. 'Never again.'

After the TV series went out, people used to stop and tell me how much they liked my floating hide. Well, my lovely people, I have to tell you that that hide will never be on telly again. After that adventure, me old mate Tony said he wanted that hide up on his farm. I brought it there, not knowing why he wanted it – it was pretty broken up by then – but when I got it there, he said, 'Johnny, you're my best mate and I don't want you to go to sea again. If you have that floating thing, you'll sure as hell try it again and drown. And I'll never see you again, which would be a great pity.'

Sadly, it wasn't long after that that Tony died suddenly, as I've said. It still hurts me to think of him saying those words. Who'd have known that he would go so quickly.

My lovely wife Julie was pleased as anything that Tony

had taken that hide. She too thought I'd drown myself in it one day. And do you know what happened to it in the end? Tony's chickens kept picking at the polystyrene, and it started to fall to pieces. Finally, when he had a clear-out in his yard, it was burnt to ashes. That was the end of my seafaring days, and a good thing too.

Some of the tales there are about the sea and the lakes and suchlike around the West Country are enough to make your hair stand on end. On Bodmin Moor, there's a lake called Dozmary Pool. It's a deep well of water and, in the old days, the locals used to swear it was bottomless. This was the lake where King Arthur threw his sword, Excalibur. He was wounded and dying, and threw his sword at his enemy, the wicked Mordred, but it went into the lake. But the beautiful Lady of the Lake rose from the water and grabbed the sword, before disappearing back down under.

There's another story about this lake too. It happened in the early 1600s. There was a magistrate called Jan Tregeagle, a very nasty man indeed. He was the cruellest man in all the West Country, and one of the richest too. The way he made his money was particularly nasty, though. He'd taken advantage of a poor orphan, robbing the child of his fortune and leaving him hungry and penniless.

After this Jan died, his ghost haunted Bodmin Moor for years. The haunting started in the same court where he'd been magistrate for all those years. There was some kind of a dispute over land which the dead man had acquired by foul deeds, and someone in the court asked Jan Tregeagle to be a witness.

Well, it was supposed to be a joke, and the people at the court fell about laughing, but they stopped soon enough when a ghostly spectre appeared in the middle of the courtroom. It was Jan Tregeagle, called out from hell. You can imagine the panic!

When everyone finally calmed down, realizing that the ghost was not going to hurt them, Jan Tregeagle told them that indeed it was him who had got the land illegally, and so it went back to its rightful owner.

The trouble was, this Tregeagle fellow was in no hurry to get back to hell, even though the demons were hounding at him, trying to get him back. He somehow managed to talk the people in the courtroom into helping him; no one knows how. Maybe he threatened to get the hounds of hell after them – who knows? Or maybe they were just nice people who felt sorry for him.

Though they promised to help Jan Tregeagle keep out of hell, they didn't want him lurking about the town either. They figured he could do as much mischief dead as he did alive. So they figured out a scheme. Old Tregeagle would be saved from hell, but he had to take on the job of emptying Dozmary Pool, with a leaking seashell.

Now, remember, you good people, that the lake was bottomless! But he had to keep going, for the deal was, if he stopped, the hounds of hell would come after him again.

This went on for years. But then one day a terrible storm came up over the lake. It was like no other storm, ever. The wind howled, the rain whipped across the lake, and the water churned up into huge, great waves. Jan Tregeagle was out of there, quick as a flash. Some stories say he fled because he was terrified of this fierce storm, but others tell that he used the weather as a way of escaping.

Whatever the reason, off he went. But, of course, as soon as he stopped trying to empty the lake, those hell demons were after him, even fiercer than the storm.

They would have got him, those demons, but Jan Tregeagle was a cunning old sod. He ran for the church which has been standing on Roche Rock since the fourteenth century. He knew that the devil couldn't get him in a Christian place, so he tried to get into that church. With the hell hounds roaring and clawing at his feet, he leaped up to get through the window of the church but, though his head got through, his shoulders – even though they were ghost shoulders! – were far too wide. He was stuck, with the demons tearing at his legs and clawing at his body.

Did that man howl with pain and terror! He howled so loud that the vicar of the parish heard him and came to the rescue. He managed to get the ghost unstuck from the church window, but then wasn't sure what to do with him. Finally, he managed to get him on to the beach at Padstow, where he gave Tregeagle another job to do to keep him out of mischief. This time, he had to weave a rope out of the sand on the beach.

Of course, this was impossible, and everyone thought that Tregeagle would spend all eternity trying to make that sand rope. But that ghost, he still had some cunning left in him. He waited for a freezing night when the temperature dropped below zero, and he poured icy water over his sand rope. It froze solid.

If Tregeagle thought he'd get away with it, and be able to roam about at his ghostly will scaring the hell out of everyone, he was dead wrong. A bunch of parsons and other holy men showed up and cast another spell on him, saying he had to go back to weaving a sand rope, only this time he wasn't allowed to go anywhere near water.

So he's there, on that beach in Padstow – other stories name other places – and you can hear his howls of rage and frustration to this day, as he tries to make a rope out of tiny grains of sand.

CHAPTER 34

A Very Special Safari

THERE SEEM TO BE A LOT OF PHEASANTS AROUND THIS YEAR, even more than usual. You can see them at the edge of the road, in fields and gardens, and all over. The cock pheasant is a beautiful bird, but he can be bad-tempered. I know a postman who was chased regularly by a pheasant. The bird used to flap about the post van on a certain country lane, and the postman knew he had to keep the windows shut when he went down that lane. One day, the pheasant was so mad that he couldn't get at the postman that he followed the man down the road and into the next drive. When the postman got out of the van, that pheasant flew at the man with such a rush that he gave a yelp and jumped a mile. The post went flying in the air any old how, most of it landing in a heap of mud from the rains the night before. That postman never did know why that cock pheasant took a particular dislike to him.

I had a pheasant take a dislike to me too, back when I was a gravedigger. I was at the village of Charles, digging a grave, and this cock pheasant couldn't leave me alone. He kept jumping right into the grave! I kept chasing him out, and back he'd come again. Once, he flew up against my shovel as I was throwing dirt out, and he got a rare old smack with that shovel, but back he came again. Another time he perched on my shovel where I'd laid it down for a minute. I picked it up, shovel and bird and all, and threw him off like he was a lump of dirt. He still came back, trying to peck me as I worked.

I was getting darned mad. Luckily, the vicar came along then, as there was a funeral, and the bird followed him right into the church when he took the coffin in. That pheasant hung on to the vicar's cloak, and he could not shake him off!

Every time there was a funeral, the pheasant did the same thing.

That pheasant hung around the church for weeks, attacking anyone who came near. He was a nasty bird, and soon got the name of Road Runner, as he was always running down the road next to the church seeing who he could attack next. Sometimes, he'd hide behind the gravestones and leap out at any unsuspecting soul who walked by.

I got to know him well, that cock pheasant. I used to try to outwit him, so I'd hide behind the gravestones myself when I saw him coming. He'd peer into the half-dug empty grave as if to say, 'Hey, Johnny, where're you to, mate? Come on out!'

I'd mutter, 'Not by a long chalk, I won't. Not until I've got something to arm myself with.' I'd find a long stick to chase him away so that I'd get my grave dug in peace. When that didn't work, I'd toss clumps of good old Devon soil at him, but still he'd come. He was one stubborn sod of a bird, that pheasant.

In the end, Road Runner turned out to be the right name for him. He died in the road, run over by a car as he was running towards the churchyard. I have to admit that I missed him when he'd gone, trouble as he was. He was some bad-tempered bird. Maybe he had troubles of his own that made him that way – who knows? But God knows, my gravedigging days at Charles were a lot easier with him gone.

All this thinking and talking and writing about old times makes me grateful that I have such good memories. Some are funny, some sad, but they're all good. Because I'm thinking about the past a lot, it seems that everything I see brings back a memory, like spotting the pheasants in the fields. I see a buzzard up in the sky, and I remember finding a baby one once and rearing it to a full-grown bird. I knew I had to let it get back into the wild, so I did. I let it out in the garden, and it flew right to the top of the house and stayed there, on top of our house, and then others in the village, for two or three days. Then, finally, off it flew, but it stayed in Bishops Nympton for about fifteen years. There was a farmer's field it particularly liked, and it flew round and round that field for years. It was good having that buzzard about.

We saw a buzzard again on a safari I took out the other day. It was a perfect day for a safari, clear and fine. There wasn't a cloud in the sky, and it was warm but with a nice breeze to keep us from getting hot. As usual, the safari started that morning when I met the folk in the car park of the school in the village. We headed out to the usual places, towards Twichen first, and along Molland Moor to Anstey Common. We saw buzzards and heard skylarks, saw rabbits and pheasants. We went Five Cross Ways through to the Barle Valley, where the deer are. We were in luck; we saw three red stags grazing down below in the valley: three young hinds. I told the group that this was a good time to see their red coats. In winter, their coats are grey; it's only in summer, when the winter coats fall out, that the strong red of the summer coats grows in. The red deer on Exmoor have been around a very long time. They are so much a part of the moor. They're still going strong – there must be over two thousand or thereabouts of them now – and with a bit of luck and care, hopefully they'll be here for many generations yet to come.

We stopped at Dulverton, the best town for shopping, then to the Moorland Mousie Trust pony centre. Here, they rescue and care for Exmoor ponies, one of the oldest wild-horse breeds in Europe.

We always see some ponies on my safaris. They are as

pretty as a picture, these animals. We are so lucky to have them roaming on the moor. We're lucky too that the Moorland Mousie Trust do a good job in helping to care for them, even though these pure-bred Exmoor ponies still live in the wild, and fend for themselves all year round. They find their own food and look after their young, and they wander free all over the moors. In the autumn, the foals and mares are herded and taken down to the farms, where they are each examined and checked over. Everyone loves to see these creatures, with their wide foreheads and large eyes. The ponies are brown or dun-coloured, with a broad back, short legs, a thick neck and a deep chest.

Living on the moor takes a good deal of stamina, and the Exmoor pony is a tough creature. It can stand the extremes of the weather up on the moor, which can be very harsh. It's got a good weatherproof coat, very important up on the moor in winter.

It's sad that the Exmoor pony is in decline after living all those centuries on the moor without any interference from us humans. Unfortunately, in the last hundred or two hundred years, so much has changed. The spread of motor vehicles, the enclosure of so much of the moor, the way farming has intensified and the so-called 'improvement' of the moor have caused the numbers to go down. But they are survivors, and they'll come through, especially with the Exmoor Pony Society and the Moorland Mousie Trust on hand to help them out. It would be a sad thing if there were no more wild ponies on Exmoor.

The Dartmoor pony is smaller than the Exmoor pony, but just as tough. It is also a rare breed, as there are only about a thousand breeding mares left. They roam wild as well. They are very gentle and make wonderful ponies for children. The Dartmoor ponies have been around since the Middle Ages. During the mining days, they were used to carry the tin from the mines. When the mines closed, the ponies were left on the moor to forage for themselves. They were also used underground, in the coal mines. They were stabled underground too, and some never saw daylight once they got to the pit. They pulled wagonloads of granite and all sorts of things over the years. They had to be strong to survive.

After seeing the ponies, I took my safari across the moor. Everyone wanted to stop now and again to look at the views, at the heather and gorse, hills and valleys. Finally, we got to Dunkery Beacon, the highest point in Somerset. We stopped there to look across the valley to Minehead, a wonderful view. The sky was so blue it looked like a painting, the trees and hills underneath a bright, clear green.

As we went zigzagging around Exmoor towards Exford, we saw warblers, a grey wagtail and a ring ouzel, which is supposed to have vanished from Exmoor – but I'm sure we saw one.

While we were spotting the birds, one of the group said, 'I know a story about a rook, Johnny, that my father used to tell when we were kids.' The man who said this was called Eric. He was on safari with his family as his seventieth-birthday present. Eric went on, 'Dad made up this verse because us kids couldn't tell the difference between a crow and a rook.'

He told it to us, and this is how it went:

> If you see a rook on its own it's a crow,
> If you see a crow in a crowd it's a rook.
> But if it's got a grey head it's a jackdaw!

We all laughed with Eric over these words. But the funny thing was, when I told it later to some of my mates, one or two of them had heard it from their own dads when they were kids. So I don't know where it comes from, but it doesn't matter. It's a good thing to remember when you get your rooks and crows mixed up! And your jackdaws as well, right?

We had a look at the river at Exford, which is very popular with the visitors, being in a pretty spot in a valley. From there, we went to Simonsbath, where we were lucky with the red deer and saw two more stags in velvet. It would take too long to list all the places we'd been to on that safari but, like all the others, it took four and a half hours. We'd gone all over Exmoor, seen deer and ponies, birds and other wildlife, and stopped at some of the most beautiful places on God's earth, like Landacre, and Tarr Steps of course, and the hills near Simonsbath. They're something special, those hills. At certain times of the year, when the light is right, they seem to have a kind of bluey tinge, like a sky at twilight. Beautiful, that.

But I could go on and on, listing all the wonderful places on Exmoor. The wonderful people, too. So many of them have helped me over the years by letting me go on their land to take photos. They know who they are, and to them I want to say a big thank you. I couldn't have done it without you, so thanks again, and God bless you all.

And now it's 10 July and I've just come home from another safari. I've got to tell you about this one, for it was magical. They're all special, but this was something else.

Sat next to me was a bloke named Paul, and in the back of the jeep was a family – a couple and their son, a youngish man. And, oh my, the things we saw! From the very beginning, that was one brilliant safari. We hadn't gone far, just out of North Molton, when we spotted a beautiful stag and about twenty or so hinds, with a young calf as well. The herd started running, and the calf ran with it so fast that, before long, it had raced past the others and was leading the race. What a sight that was.

From there, we went to Twichen, for this Paul had seen my programmes on the telly and wanted to see where Tony was buried. They also wanted to meet Albert, because they'd seen him on the programme too. It pleased me, you know, that people remembered Tony and Albert. Albert was happy too, because he and Tony were best mates, and I know he likes the chance to talk about him now he's gone.

Two good mates of mine, one gone and the other

hopefully around for a long time yet! Did'ya hear that, Albert? You stick around, my friend! Tony wouldn't want you to join him yet, I know.

The next exciting thing that happened was up towards Dulverton, up to Draydon Rails. We were on a narrow road, not much traffic, and I was going slow. Suddenly, we saw a stoat, carrying a rabbit nearly twice as big as he was. Would you believe, this stoat walked right in front of us. I'd parked the jeep at the side of the road and, as we watched, this stoat walked about 80 foot, carrying this big old rabbit in his mouth. When he got to about a yard in front of us, he dropped the rabbit and looked right at us. Can you believe it? It was like he was saying, Have a good look then, I don't mind. As long as you don't take my dinner! Then he picked up the rabbit and ran off with it.

What a sight that was. We needed an ice cream after that, so we went to my ice-cream man Paul at Tarr's Steps, who sells the best ice creams in the world. I bought everyone a Honeycomb ice cream. We sat eating our ice creams, looking at the river, without a care in the world.

We went on our way, happy as larks. And luck was still with us when we went up Winsford Hill and, suddenly, a red kite flew right over us. I couldn't believe it. I've only seen three in the last five years, and here was one gliding right over us, letting us have a good look at him. What a sight that was. The red kite is a bird of prey with a wing span of over six and a half feet. He got close enough for us to see his forked tail, and that brilliant chestnutty-red colour.

And that wasn't all. We got to the top of the hill near Dunkery Beacon, and there in front of us were a herd of about sixty deer, with ten small calves. Oh, it was a rare old sight, and we just stared. Straight in front of us, as if those deer were there just for this: to be there for us to see. It was bloody brilliant.

And then, of all things, after such a beautiful day, the sky got black as coal and the heavens opened and it started pouring with rain. But nobody minded. We'd had a fantastic safari. When we got back I told everyone that I wanted to write about that safari in my new book, so that's what I'm doing now. It was something special, and I'll never forget it.

CHAPTER 35

The Emperor

THE SUMMER IS OVER NOW, AND AUTUMN IS STARTING. I'VE finished my filming, and the programmes on birds are about to be shown on BBC4. It's my busiest time of year, with the stags rutting. Everyone wants to go on safari to see that.

But something has happened which upset me very much this year. It was to do with one of the great stags of Exmoor, called the Emperor. There have been so many misunderstandings and half-true stories told in the press about my involvement in this incident that I'd like to tell it to you now, the way it really happened.

I knew the Emperor very well. I'd filmed his father, Bruno, for many years. And I'd filmed the son for the last four years.

The Emperor was getting old, and near the end of his time. I'd seen him fighting another stag, a rough looking thing, but younger. The Emperor lost the fight and was moved away to other land.

The night before the Emperor was shot, I heard him roaring. I was out, and I heard him, you couldn't mistake it.

I went out at 7 a.m. on 8 October, down to the woods with some people who wanted to see the stags. At 7.20, I heard one shot, ten seconds later, I heard another. I got the folk with me out of the way, not knowing where the shooting was coming from. Then I ran back to my truck, puffing like mad, and drove to the North Devon link road. I came to a lay-by on the left-hand side and pulled in to have a look. On the opposite side of the road there was another lay-by and there was a white van and a lorry in it, with two men who were looking down into the field.

It was very foggy, so I couldn't see their faces clearly. One of them had a pair of field glasses and the other had something that looked like a camera with a long lens. I picked up my Swarovski field glasses and, looking down the same way to the field, I could see that a stag was lying on the grass and, from the size of its antlers, that it was a big stag. I had seen enough, so I drove the short distance up the road to the next junction with the intention of turn-ing my vehicle around and heading back to the people I was with.

Before I could do that, this vehicle approached me and the man said, 'Hello, Johnny.' I was wondering how he knew who I was, but, of course, my name was on the side of my truck. I could see that he was a deerstalker by the way he was dressed and I said, 'I hope you've not just shot the Emperor.' He looked at me and said, 'What do you take me for?' I replied, 'I don't even know you,' and then he just drove away. I'm not for a moment pointing the finger and saying that either of them did shoot the Emperor, I'm just telling it as it happened that morning.

Then I made my way back to the estate to see my people and broke the news that I thought the Emperor was dead. The business wasn't anything to do with me. The Emperor was old, even though he was still a magnificent stag. He was nearly 8 feet tall and weighed over 300lbs. But I know that the old stags have to give way to the new. If the man who shot it had permission from the owners of the land to shoot on it, then it was all legal and above board. Anyway, it wasn't my concern.

Three days later, all hell broke loose. The phone kept ringing, with the press asking questions, wanting to know what I thought of the Emperor being shot. On Sunday morning – at 9.30 a.m., would you believe? – there was a man from one of the national newspapers at my door. He didn't take kindly to it when I said that Sunday morning was supposed to be our family day at home.

The newspapers started printing all sorts of untrue stories. Because I'd taken a photo of the Emperor only four days before he died – I was the last man to do so – I was accused both of making up the story and of shooting him myself to increase the ratings for my programme. The story went on and on in the media. Many of the things said about me were lies, and very hurtful, to both me and Julie, my wife. The whole thing went out of control because of the name: the Emperor. Every year, old stags are culled and no one takes any notice, but because this one carried a name, a big story was made out of it.

Nobody made this much of a fuss when Bruno was found dead, twelve years ago, on the same day as the Emperor. Now that stag was a character. He came from Rackenford. He had huge antlers, with all his rights, meaning brow, bay and tray on each antler with seven and eight points on the top, but he was palm-headed, as they say; that is, his antlers had started deteriorating.

Last year, the Emperor's points were better than this year. I noticed this when I photographed him. The Emperor was deteriorating. Now, I don't say this in a sad way, but in a kind way. You see, the Emperor had lived a good life, and done his duty, siring many youngsters. But he was now palm-headed. He was getting old, he was declining. It's nature; it's what happens.

Bruno, the Emperor's father, was also past his prime when he was found dead. Everyone knew that stag. The hunting people were told not to touch him, and they didn't. When they were out hunting around Rackenford, they knew to look out for Bruno, and leave him alone.

It was the same thing with the Emperor. The hunt people respected this. This was another reason there was such a fuss made when the Emperor was killed, because there was an understanding that this stag should be left alone as well.

But Bruno, he was some stag, big and powerful. I was very lucky to be able to film him. This was because of the kindness of two very nice ladies who owned the land where Bruno roamed much of the time. They gave me permission to film on their land. I was honoured that they let me do this, and I got some great shots of him.

That stag could be scary, though. He had the deepest roar I've ever known on a stag. More than once he went after me when I was trying to film him. Once, I was in the woods when Bruno came roaring in. It was rutting season and, let me tell you, a magnificent stag in rut is a fearsome sight. I got up a tree and stayed for two and a half hours, waiting for him to get bored with scaring old Johnny Kingdom and go away.

He was some animal, and so was the Emperor. And I'm sure there will be another stag somewhere that will be a real animal but become something of a legend with time, just like the Emperor.

The red deer that roam Exmoor are wonderful creatures, as I've mentioned before. No wonder that so many pubs are named after stags. Long ago, in ancient times, the stag was considered one of the gods of the woodland. It was thought to bring good things to whoever saw it. Maybe that was because of those huge antlers.

There was also a strange tradition in Devon around a stag hunt that wasn't exactly a stag hunt, for no deer were involved in it. This took place in various towns in mid-

Devon sometime in the mid-1800s. It seemed to be a way of casting shame on people in the village who had done something wrong.

The way it went was like this. The leader of the 'stag' hunt dressed up in antlers and some kind of deer get-up. Then he started to run. The 'huntsmen' and 'hounds' were the people of the town, who started chasing the 'stag' in and out amongst the streets. You can imagine all the hollering and yelling and excitement. Everyone joined in, even the children.

Finally, the man who was playing the stag got to the house of the person or people who were the victims. Now, this lot weren't part of the game; they were the ones who were being shamed by the rest of the village. The hunters and hounds pretended to attack and kill the stag right on the doorsteps of those poor victims. In one town – Okehampton, I believe it was – the 'stag' took out an ox bladder he'd been carrying and dropped it on the doorstep, to get it all bloody. It was a very clear message to those inside the house. They'd been spotted doing something the townspeople disapproved of, and they had better mend their ways, or worse would come. It was a dire warning, enough to put the fear of God up anyone, I would imagine.

In some of the smaller villages dotted around this part of Devon, there were variations of this stag hunt. In one place, it got a bit nasty. Any man suspected of going after a married woman while her husband was away working in the fields or suchlike was hunted down by the pretend hounds and chased until he died of a heart attack, or exposure from being thrown into a river on a freezing wintry night.

One village did it with a lot of noise. All the men met, with pans to bang on, bells to ring, drums, whatever, to make as much of a din as possible. They charged through the village to their victim's house. This was someone who had done something against the rules of the place, such as stealing a sheep, or whatever. Taking the law into their own hands, the villagers charged the wrongdoer's house, clanging their pots and pans and shouting until they forced the person out. Then the leader put on a pair of antlers, or sometimes a ram's horns. They gave the poor harassed man a head start, then the crowd ran after him, howling like hounds. When they finally caught him, they threw him in a stream or a pool of water and then left him to his fate. Usually, he dragged himself home and, if he had any sense, never stole another sheep or whatever in his life. The 'stag's hunt' had been a warning. He wouldn't get another chance.

That's one custom I'm glad has died away. It sounds too much like mob rule to me.

Stags like the Emperor, and Bruno, his father, have become legend because of their size and strength and character. There have been others, and there will be more. I feel honoured that I've had the chance to get to know those two stags, and to film them. I hope there will be others like it before I'm too old to hold a camera.

Julie comes into my office while I'm thinking about the Emperor. I tell her that I'm setting it all down on paper, to tell it like it happened, and she says she's pleased.

But then I forget about the stags, about filming, about everything else, as our granddaughter Roxy comes into the room. She's holding a baby in her arms, her firstborn, and not even a month old yet. Julie coos at the baby, then looks at me and smiles. It's our very first great-grandchild: a lovely little boy. What an amazing way to end a fantastic year!

I feel over the moon about the baby: a new life, a new person to carry on the stories, pass on the old traditions, the myths and legends we've been handed down by our ancestors. And to make new ones too. New tales, new stories. The old ones will last but there'll be many more as well. That's how it's always been, and always will be.

Acknowledgements

This book would not have been written without the help of a wonderful man I met many years ago. He passed away a couple of years ago, but I would like to tell you about him.

Years ago, I was very ill with a breakdown, after a terrible accident I had with a tractor when I was a tree feller. The doctors couldn't do any more for me. They suggested I see a man called the Revd Pennington, who was a local vicar.

An appointment was made for me to go to the vicarage and meet Revd Pennington at North Molton. I knocked on the door, and a tall man opened it. He had swept-back hair, wore glasses, and had a very kind voice. He started talking to me. 'Hello, Johnny. They tell me you are not well.'

'Yes, sir,' I replied.

'Well, we will try and make you better. I understand you smoke a lot of cigarettes a day, is that right? How many?'

'Well, sir,' I said, 'sometimes sixty or more a day.'

'Oh dear.' He shook his head. 'I can't stop you altogether, but I will try my best to cut you down a bit.'

This was my first day with this good man. I didn't know what to expect. He asked me to sit down in an armchair, and put my left hand on my knee. So I did. Then he said, 'Now take it off again.' But I could not. It was like someone had stuck it there.

He looked at me and said, 'Your sixty cigarettes are now down to thirty a day.' I was puzzled. He said, 'Look at me again.' He counted 1–2–3, and my hand came off my knee, just like that, so easy.

That was the first time. I was puzzled, but I trusted him, so I came back again. The second night, I knocked on the door and this kind man was waiting for me. 'Come in, Johnny, sit down. How do you feel?'

'A bit better,' I said. It was true.

'Well done. Tonight is going to be a bit different.'

'OK, sir.'

'Please sit down in the big armchair again.'

'OK, sir.'

He waited until I was settled in the chair. 'Right,' he said, 'do you ever go to sleep in a chair?'

'Yes, sir,' I replied.

'OK. Show me how.'

I put my hand against my head. 'Like this,' I said.

'OK, Johnny. Relax.'

He walked towards me and put his hand on my head. He said some very kind words about our God – or Jesus, if you like – and the next thing I remember was waking up very sleepy, like I was coming around from a good night on the cider.

He said these words: 'Johnny, you have not been to sleep. I took you back to the age of five.'

I said, 'What?!' In my mind, I was wondering what the hell was going on here. I wondered what I was doing there.

But something was changing in me. That man was healing me.

I saw Revd Pennington only three times, but close together. After that second time, I walked out the door and tried to have a fag, or cigarette if you like. I lit it and had one puff. It was so bad that I threw it out of my truck window to the floor.

I got out mad as an adder, and stamped on it. If anyone had seen me they would have thought I'd gone crazy.

But the smoking was gone for good. Not only that, but all the Valium tablets were gone too. That vicar had given me a new start in life. I was a new man.

Years went by, but my heart never forgot that wonderful man. I became famous with the TV programmes and started giving talks to people in all sorts of places. Thirty years on from that time with the Revd Pennington, I found him again. We'd gone our separate ways and had lost touch, but something inside me wanted to see him one more time.

Then someone told me that he was still alive and living

in a home at Bridgerule in Cornwall. I went off straight-away to see him.

It was a Sunday morning. I knocked on the door of that home, and some lovely ladies came to the door and welcomed me in, saying they were fans of mine. We had a good old chat together and then went to Revd Pennington's room. He was sitting in a chair, fast asleep. I got a chair and sat beside his bed. He woke up, looked at me and said, 'Hello, Johnny. How are you?' Just like that – after all those years!

'Fine, sir,' I said. We had a cup of tea together. Then he said, 'What time is it, Johnny? Because I've got to get to church to take the service.'

I said, 'No, sir. You have done your part in church. Now you must rest.'

He looked at me and gave me such a lovely smile. Then I had to go. I said, 'Cheerio,' and he waved and said the same. I didn't like to say goodbye. He was coming up for his ninety-eighth birthday then, and later his daughter told me that he had a wonderful birthday. But shortly after that he passed away, in peace.

I went to the funeral at Hartland. It was a wonderful service, with an oil painting of him standing right in front of his coffin, in front of the altar. I went to the graveside and saw him put to rest with his lovely wife. I stood on the steep ground looking down and, after his family all walked away from the graveside, I went down and stood on my own. Because, you see, I had a few words to say to him, looking down into his grave. I said, 'Dear Lord take this lovely man and his wife and keep them safe. This message is from me and my wife, Julie. Thank you for your help. Rest in peace.'

So you see, that's why I keep telling everyone about this man. Without him, I wouldn't have started my new life. I'll never forget him, as long as I live.

This is why I am telling you lovely people. Please, if you are not well, don't give up, because there is someone that may help you. Someone, somewhere, just like the Revd Pennington helped me.

As well as saying a big thank you to Julie and all my wonderful family, and to all the friends and well-wishers who have supported me in my work, I would like to add a big thank you to the people who have sponsored me. They are Devonshire Mitsubishi Motors in Barnstaple; Jack Pike for the best camouflage gear; and Swarovski for the excellent field glasses. I'm very grateful to all of you.

And finally, I would like to say a special thank you to Graham Cripps, my dentist, who recommended Ian Mills and his team at his practice in Torrington. Ian has just done my four implants for me and he made the whole thing as worry-free as it could have been. I would recommend him to anyone.

About the Author

Johnny Kingdom lives on the edge of Exmoor with his wife, Julie. For the past several years he has made a living running wildlife safaris on the moor and making videos of its flora and fauna. Johnny became a local celebrity with a nature series on ITV West but is now a national treasure following his BBC2 series and Christmas specials.